Finger Fitness for Pianists

---

200 Exercises to Stay in Shape, Avoid Injury, and Sound Fabulous

Jim Stopher, D.M.A.

Overture Music Press

Finger Fitness for Pianists:
200 Exercises to Stay in Shape, Avoid Injury,
and Sound Fabulous

ISBN: 979-8-9926735-2-4

© 2025 Overture Music Press. All rights reserved.

Introduction

Who is this book for?
This text is for pianists who want to improve or maintain their technique in a structured, efficient, and enjoyable way. A solid technical routine sharpens skills, prevents injury, and enables repertoire playing to be more comfortable and gratifying.

How this book is organized
Inside are 200 exercises, grouped into 5 workouts of 40 exercises each.

Each **exercise**:
- is exactly 1 page long
- is easy to learn and fun to play
- is fully notated and fingered
- lists metronome marks from beginner to advanced
- trains the two hands equally.

Each **workout**:
- can be completed in about 25 minutes
- addresses a wide variety of techniques, including bedrock skills like scales and arpeggios
- uses all common key signatures, up to 6 sharps or flats
- has a logical progression from one exercise to the next
- is satisfying to play as a unit.

How to practice
This collection is designed to be flexible and useful to beginner, intermediate, and advanced pianists.

Beginner pianists can learn the initial exercises of Workout #1 at the slower metronome marks, then progress gradually through the remaining exercises to build stamina, speed, and technique.

Intermediate pianists can aim to master all five workouts at the upper end of the given metronome ranges, then institute a habit of playing through one workout per day.

Advanced pianists can use this book as a convenient way to stay in shape, playing at or above the highest metronome marks, and going through two or more workouts per day.

All pianists can peruse the whole set and select individual exercises they find particularly helpful to incorporate into their practice sessions.

Notes on the Exercises

These exercises are designed to be **practical** and **immediately applicable** to the standard repertoire. In fact, many are inspired by specific passages in the literature. For example:
- Workout #1 Exercise 16 (p. 17) uses the fingering for trills in thirds from Mendelssohn's *Rondo capriccioso*.
- Workout #4 Exercise 38 (p. 165) was prompted by the stretches in Chopin's Étude, Op. 25, No. 1.
- Workout #5 Exercise 23 (p. 192) mimics a double note figure from the finale of Beethoven's Piano Sonata, Op. 10, No. 2.

Within each workout, the exercises are grouped into **families** of 2-5 pages. Each family has a technical theme and progresses in difficulty.

The **dynamic level** is *fortissimo* throughout. Practicing technical exercises loudly maximizes gains and makes it easier to play softly when working on repertoire.

Dexterity exercises train all five fingers of each hand for speed and evenness.
- Each workout begins with a family inspired by Hanon's *The Virtuoso Pianist*, but in keys other than C major to challenge the fingers and the mind.
- Later in each workout, there is a dexterity family in which each hand spans an octave.
- Each workout concludes with a focus on extended positions, where each hand spans more than an octave.

Stability exercises condition the fingers not to collapse when using significant arm weight.

Crossover exercises address two fundamental challenges of scale and arpeggio playing: passing the thumb under the hand, and crossing other fingers over the thumb.

Scale and arpeggio families include preparatory stability and crossover exercises before moving to one- and two-octave drills. Pay close attention to the fingering, as these exploit the difficulty of thumb passes.

Ornament exercises train the fingers for speed in shorter bursts, aiding with the clean execution of mordents, turns, and trills.

Other **specialty exercises** prepare skills called for in virtuosic music, like sixths, large chords, and repeated notes.

Table of Contents

Workout #1

Exercises	Techniques	Keys	Page
1-5	Dexterity in close positions	D, E♭, E, F, F♯	2
6-8	Stability for individual fingers	A, B, D♭	7
9-10	Crossovers	C, C	10
11-14	Major scales	All major	12
15-17	Thirds	C, C, B♭	16
18-19	Broken four-note major chords	All major	19
20-23	Ornaments	B, G, G♭, A♭	21
24-26	Staccato octaves	All major and minor, A	25
27-30	Dexterity in octave positions	C, C, C, C	28
31-34	Major arpeggios	All major	32
35-37	Harmonized octaves	C, all major	36
38-40	Dexterity in extended positions	D, D♭, C	39

Workout #2

Exercises	Techniques	Keys	Page
1-5	Dexterity in close positions	E♭, E, F, G♭, G	44
6-8	Stability for individual fingers	E, D♭, C	49
9-10	Crossovers	C, C	52
11-14	Natural minor scales	All minor	54
15-17	Sixths	C, D, C	58
18-20	Polyphonic figures	C, F♯, B♭	61
21-23	Repeated notes	A, A♭, G	64
24-26	Broken octaves	All major and minor	67
27-30	Dexterity in octave positions	C, C, C, C	70
31-34	Minor arpeggios	All minor	74
35-37	Four-note chords	C, all major, C	78
38-40	Dexterity in extended positions	C, B, C	81

Workout #3

Exercises	Techniques	Keys	Page
1-5	Dexterity in close positions	E, F, F♯, G, A♭	86
6-8	Stability for two fingers	C, C, C	91
9-10	Crossovers	D, B♭	94
11-14	The chromatic scale	All	96
15-18	Thirds	A, D♭, all major	100
19-20	Broken four-note minor chords	All minor	104
21-23	Ornaments	G♭, B, F	106
24-26	The chromatic scale in octaves	All	109
27-30	Dexterity in octave positions	C, C, C, C	112
31-34	Dominant seventh arpeggios	All major	116
35-37	Harmonized octaves	C, all major	120
38-40	Dexterity in extended positions	D♭, E♭, C	123

Workout #4

Exercises	Techniques	Keys	Page
1-5	Dexterity in close positions	F, G♭, G, A♭, A	128
6-8	Stability for two fingers	C, C, C	133
9-10	Thumb underneath the hand	B, C	136
11-14	Harmonic minor scales	All minor	138
15-17	Sixths	C, all major, C	142
18-19	Broken five-note chords	All minor	145
20-22	Legato octaves	D, E♭, E	147
23-26	Double-note figures	All major, B♭	150
27-30	Dexterity in octave positions	C, C, C, C	154
31-34	Diminished seventh arpeggios	All	158
35-37	Four-note chords	All minor, c	162
38-40	Dexterity in extended positions	F♯, D♭, C	165

Workout #5

Exercises	Techniques	Keys	Page
1-5	Dexterity in close positions	D♭, D, E♭, E, F	170
6-8	Stability for three fingers	C, C, C	175
9-10	Thumb underneath the hand	A, B♭	178
11-14	Melodic minor scales	All minor	180
15-17	Thirds	C, F♯, c	184
18-19	Ornaments	G, A♭	187
20-21	Three-note chords	All major	189
22-23	Double-note figures	B, G♭	191
24-26	Staccato octaves	All major and minor	193
27-30	Dexterity in octave positions	C, C, C, C	196
31-34	Major seventh arpeggios	All major	200
35-37	Large chords	All major	204
38-40	Dexterity in extended positions	All major, A, C	207

About the Author

Jim Stopher maintains an active career as a conductor, pianist, composer, and educator. He is chair of the music department at the College of Marin (California), where he teaches courses in music theory, repertoire, and musicianship. He is also music director of the College of Marin Symphony Orchestra and the Marin Symphony Youth Orchestra. Jim earned degrees at Harvard University (BA), the University of Arizona (MM), and the Peabody Conservatory (DMA).

Workout #1

— Workout #1 —

Dexterity exercise emphasizing a 4-5 stretch in the LH (ascending) and RH (descending).

1.

— Workout #1 —

Dexterity exercise. Play legato throughout, including from measure to measure.

Workout #1

Dexterity exercise emphasizing 4-note scale fragments.

— Workout #1 —

Dexterity exercise with frequent changes of direction.

Dexterity exercise focusing on the weaker fingers of the RH (ascending) and LH (descending).

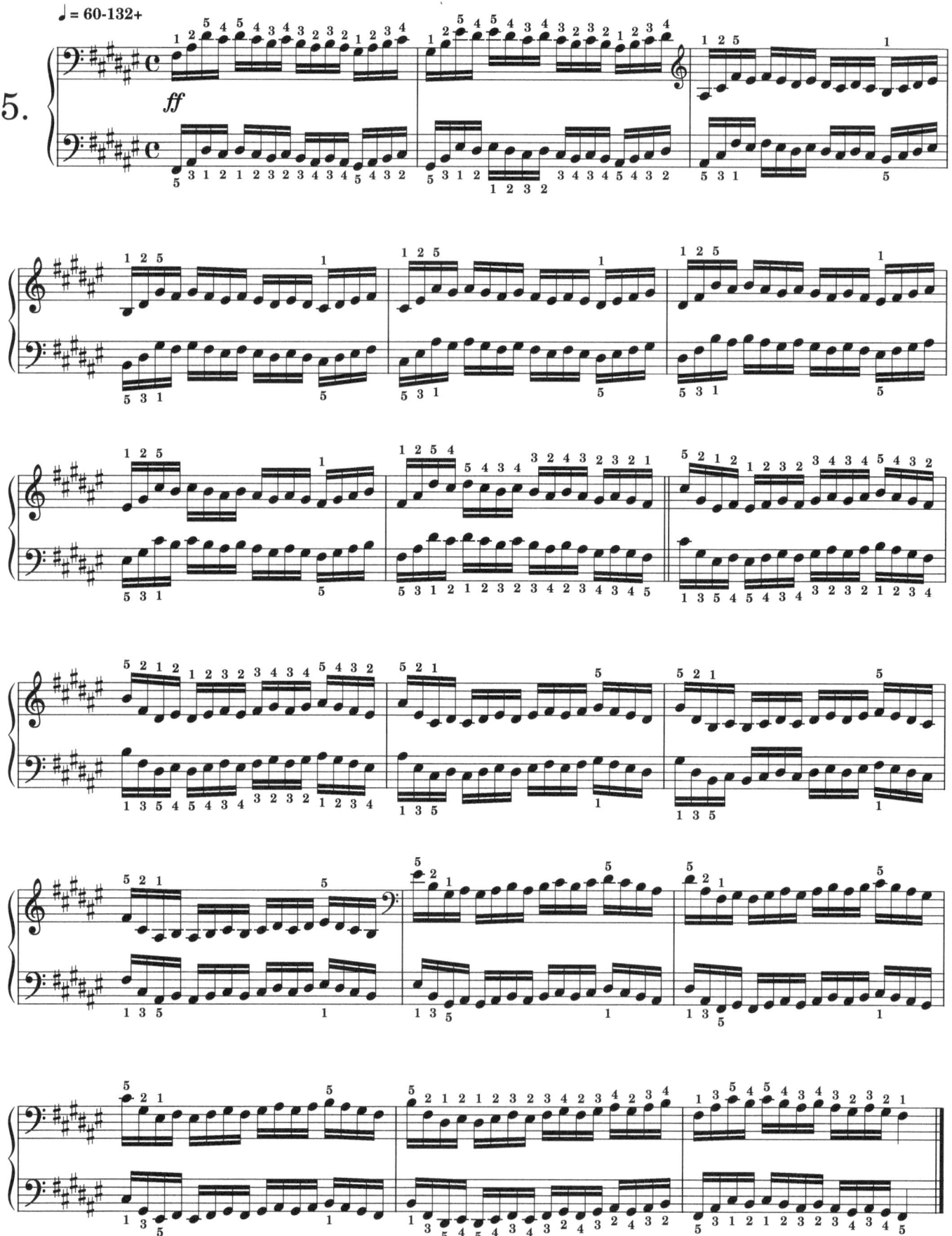

Stability exercise: use only the thumbs throughout.

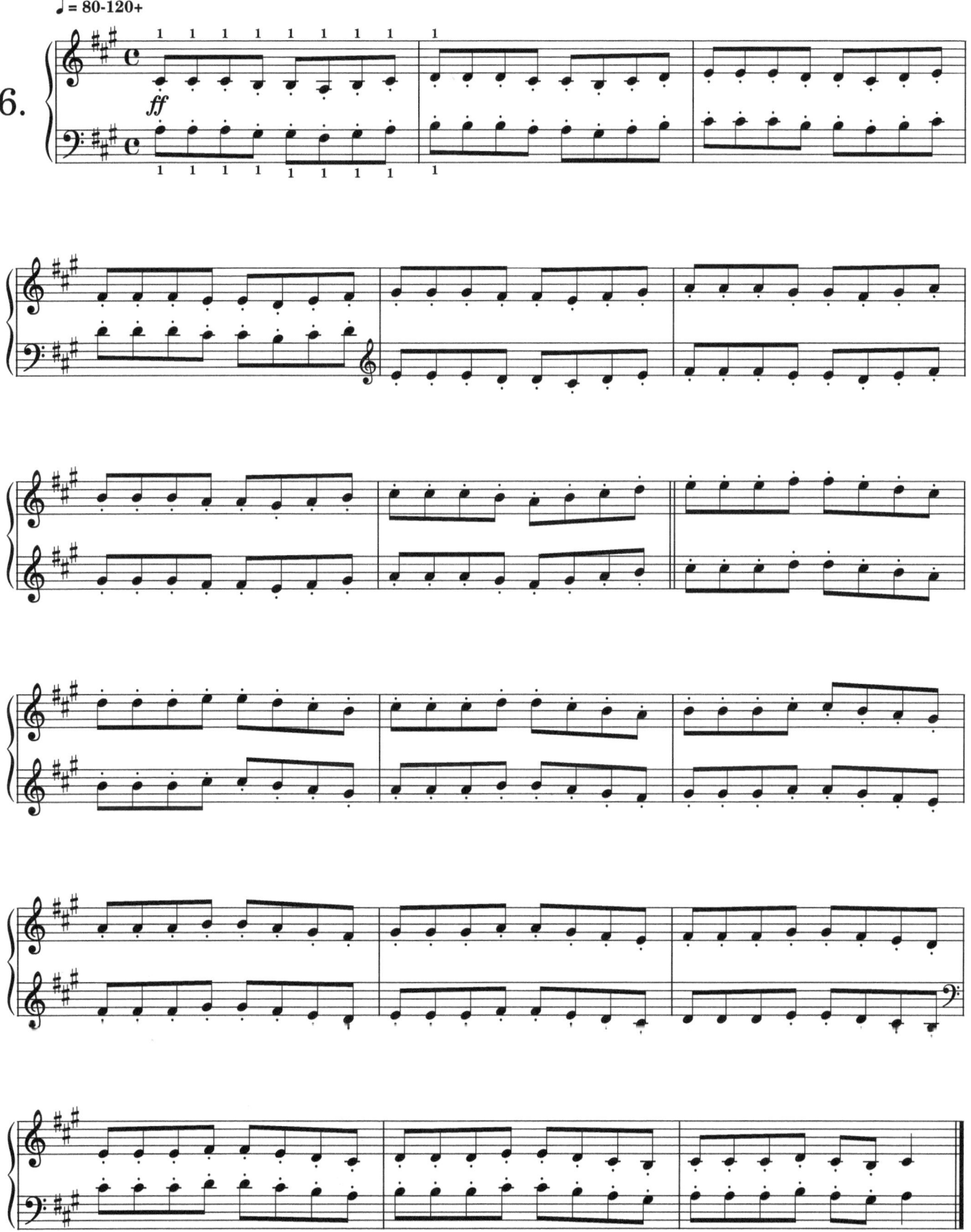

— Workout #1 —

Stability exercise: use only the 2nd finger of each hand throughout.

— Workout #1 —

Stability exercise: use only the 3rd finger of each hand throughout.

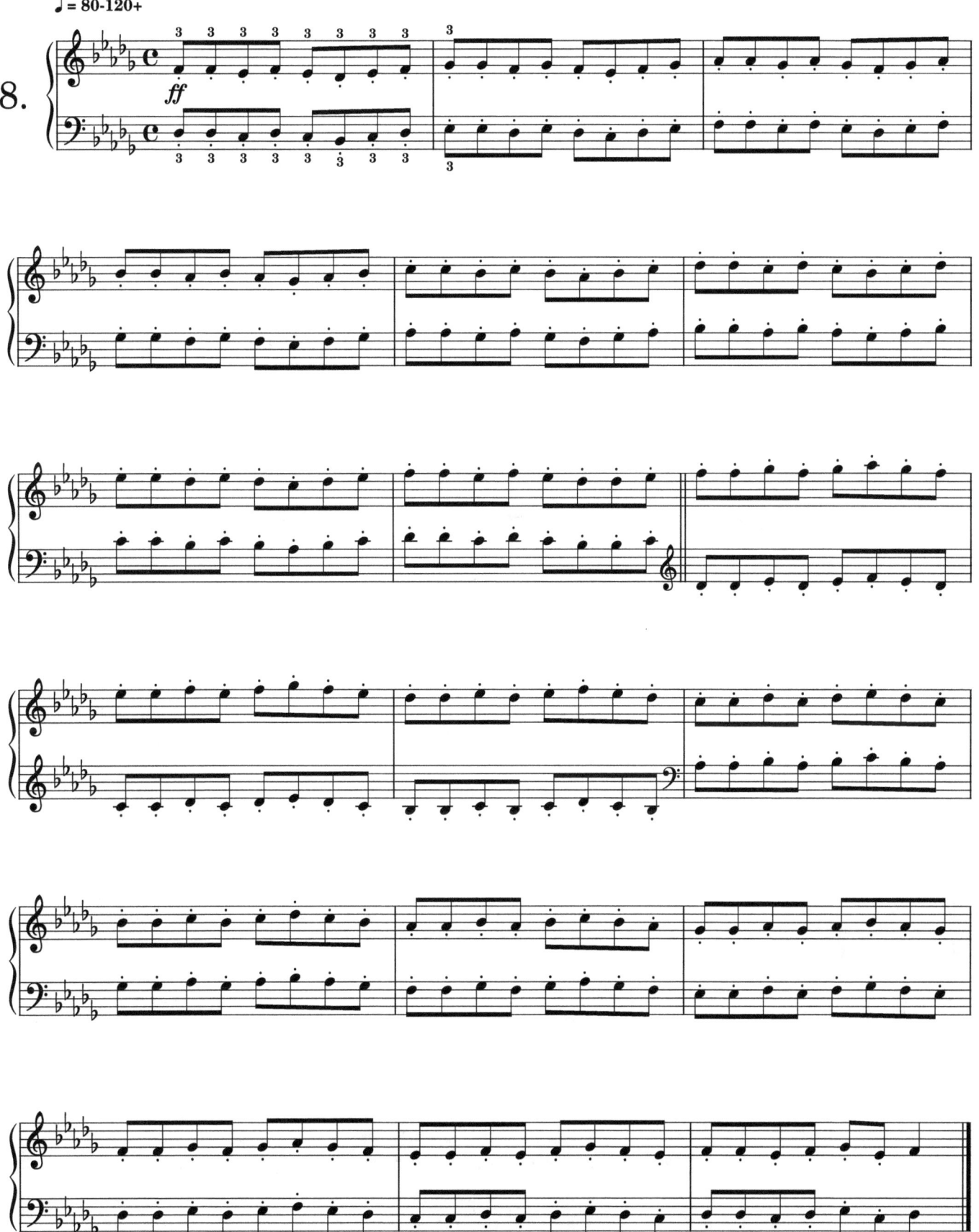

8.

Exercise for crossing the 2nd finger over the thumb.

— Workout #1 —

Exercise for crossing the 3rd finger over the thumb.

— Workout #1 —

Stability preparation for all major scales. Follow the fingering carefully.

— Workout #1 —

Crossover preparation for all major scales. Follow the fingering carefully.

— Workout #1 —

One-octave major scales. Follow the fingering carefully.

— Workout #1 —

Two-octave major scales. Follow the fingering carefully.

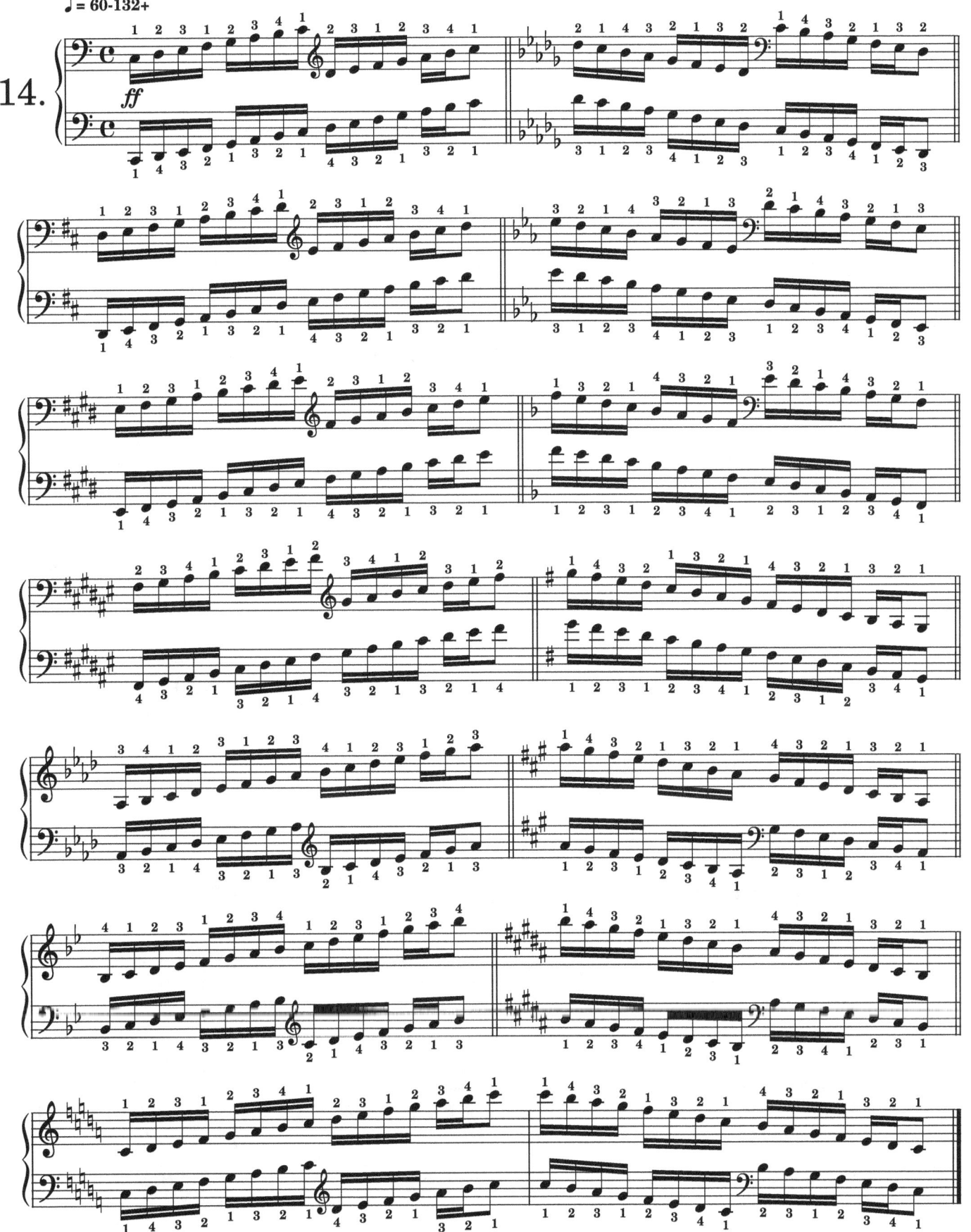

— Workout #1 —

Exercise for thirds using 3-4-5 in the outer voices. Play all 16th notes legato.

Trill figure in thirds. Play all 16th notes legato.

— Workout #1 —

Thirds exercise using 2-3-4-5 in the outer voices. Play the 16th notes as legato as possible. (Consecutive thumb notes will be slightly separated.)

— Workout #1 —

Broken 4-note major triads in root position, 1st inversion, and 2nd inversion.

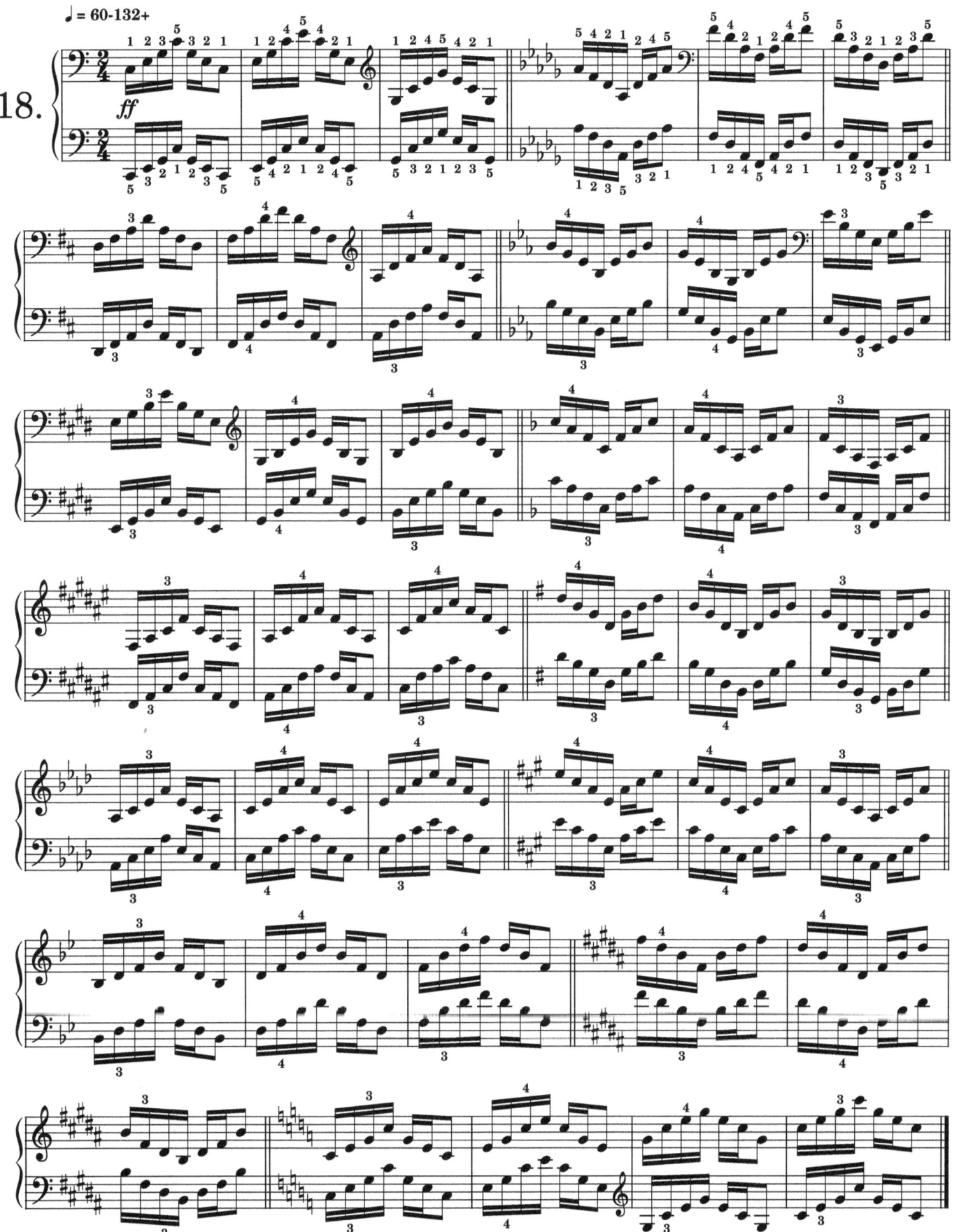

— Workout #1 —

Broken 4-note major triads. Each measure contains root position, 1st inversion, and 2nd inversion.

— Workout #1 —

Mordent exercise using all adjacent finger pairs.

— Workout #1 —

Exercise for short trills beginning on the main note. Ensure the LH keeps pace with the RH.

— Workout #1 —

Exercise for a common turn figure. Pay close attention to fingers 3, 4, and 5.

— Workout #1 —

Exercise for short trills beginning on the upper note.

— Workout #1 —

All major scales in octaves. Use the 5th finger on white keys and the 4th on black keys.

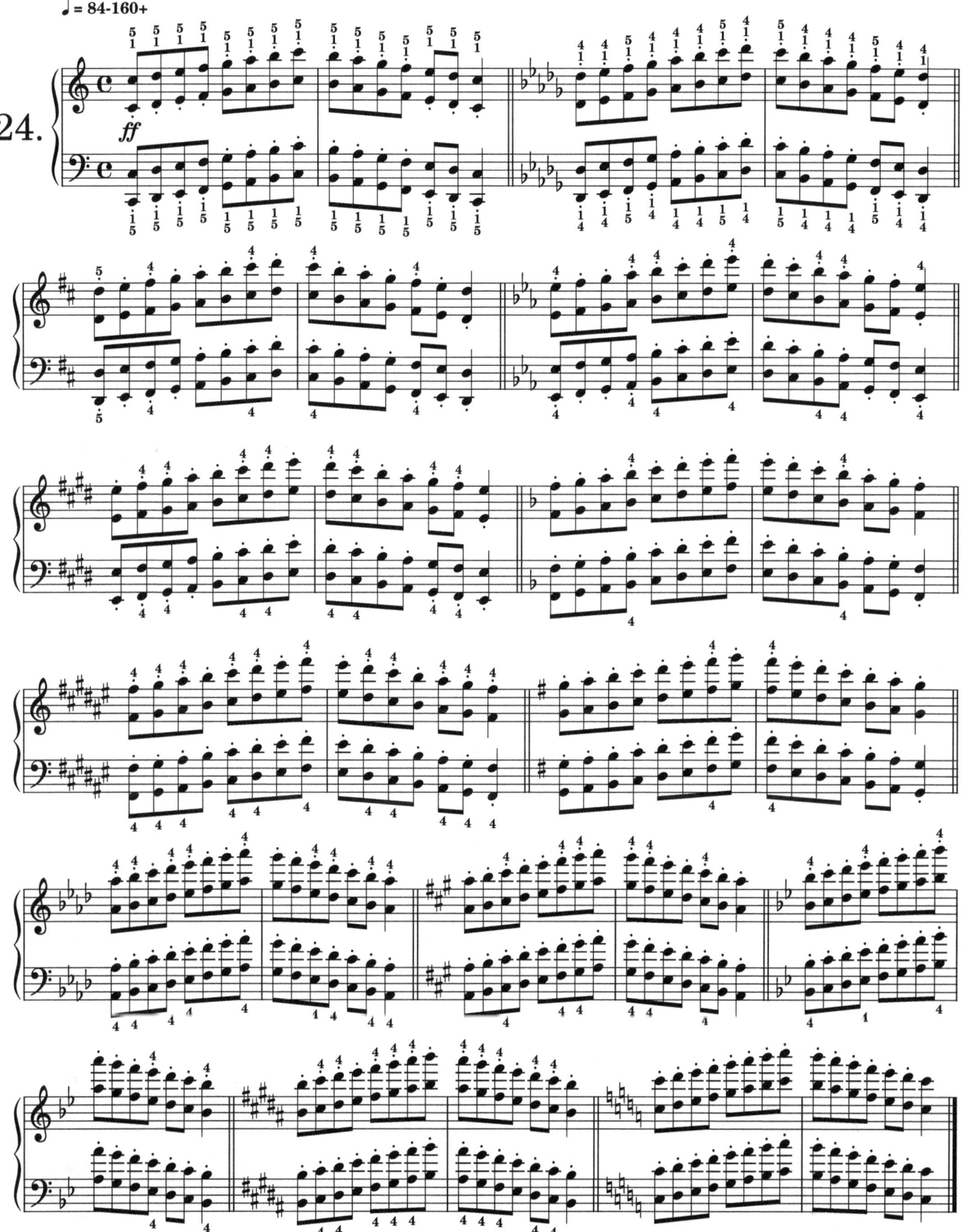

— Workout #1 —

All harmonic minor scales in octaves. Continue using the 4th finger on black keys.

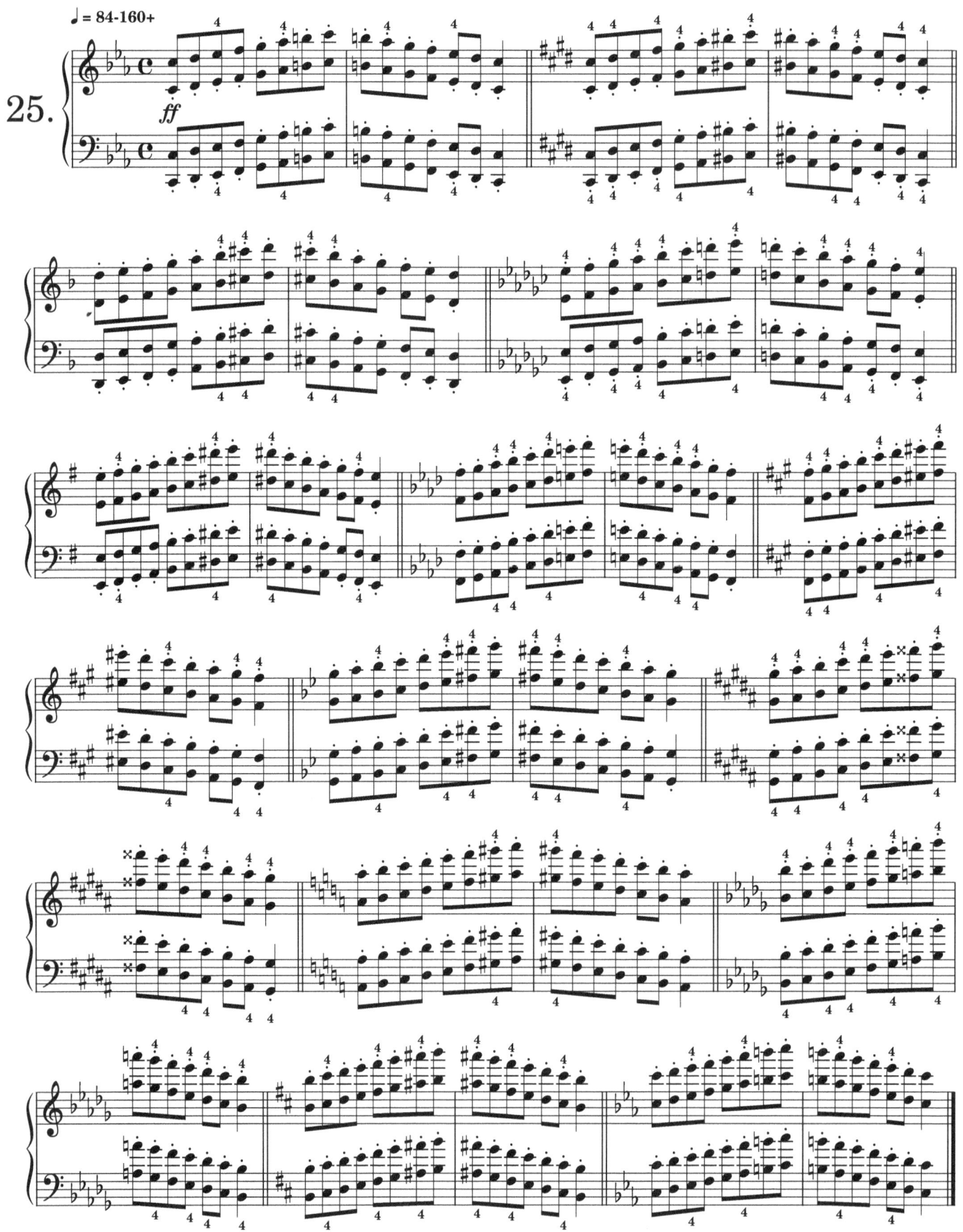

— Workout #1 —

Staccato octaves with more frequent changes of direction. Use the 4th finger on black keys.

— Workout #1 —

Dexterity exercise with emphasis on scale fragments.

28

— Workout #1 —

Dexterity exercise with emphasis on fingers 3, 4, and 5 in the RH (ascending) and LH (descending).

— Workout #1 —

Dexterity exercise beginning with a trill figure.

29.

Workout #1

Dexterity exercise with emphasis on 4-note broken chords.

♩ = 60-132+

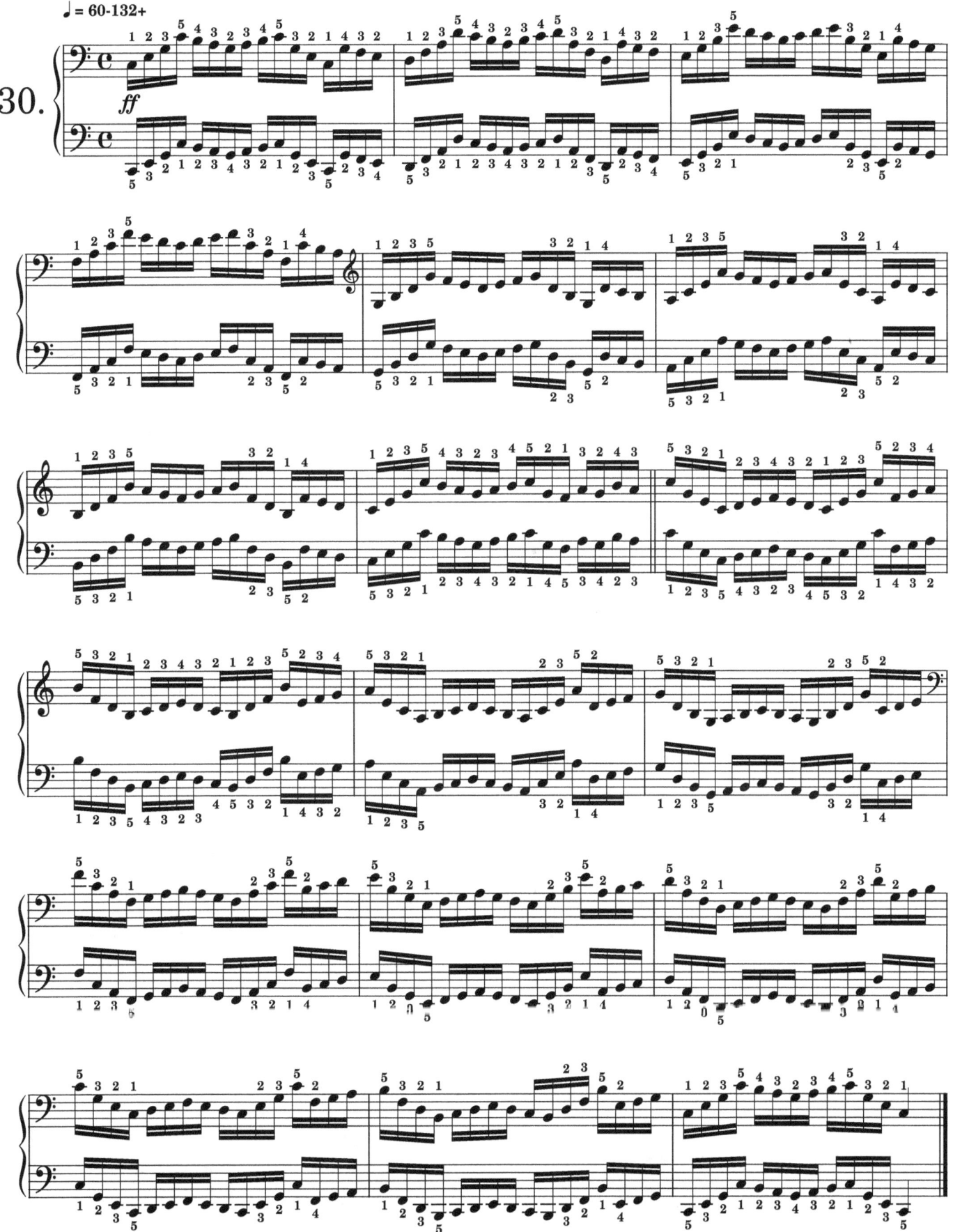

30.

ff

Stability preparation for major arpeggios. Follow the fingering carefully.

— Workout #1 —

Crossover preparation for major arpeggios. Follow the fingering carefully.

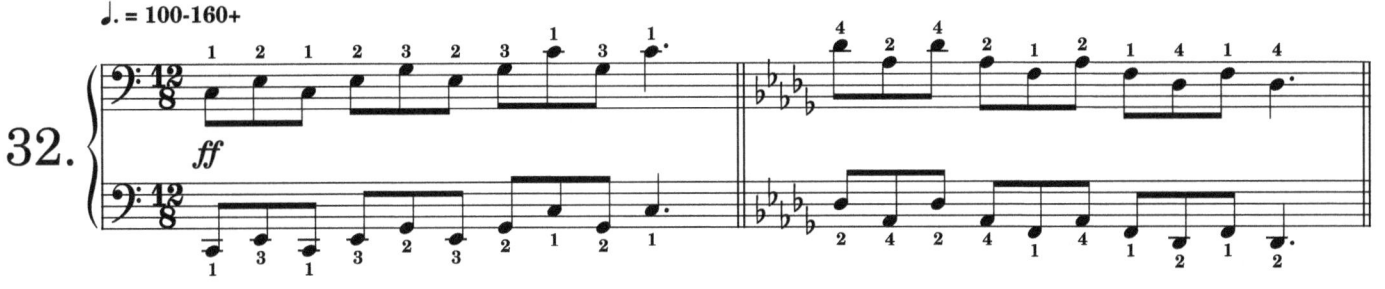
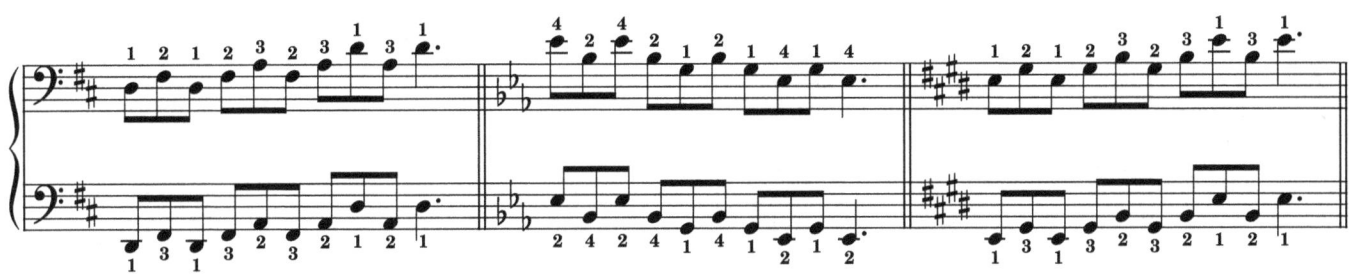

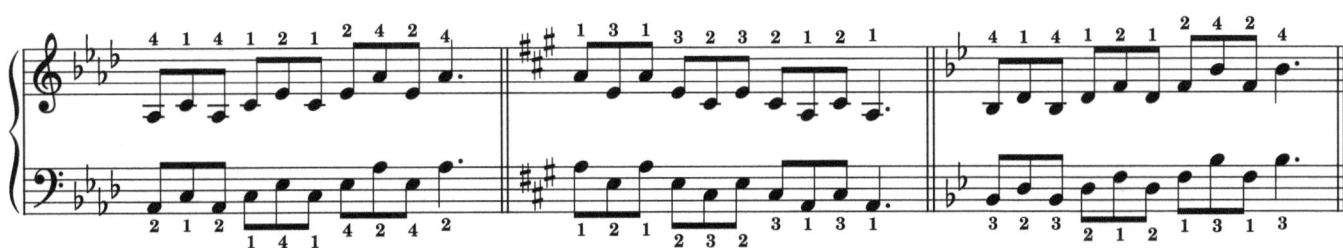
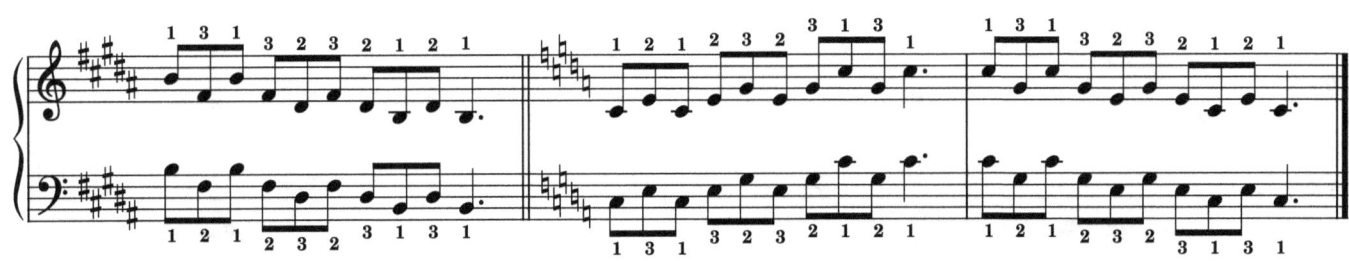

One-octave major arpeggios. Follow the fingering carefully.

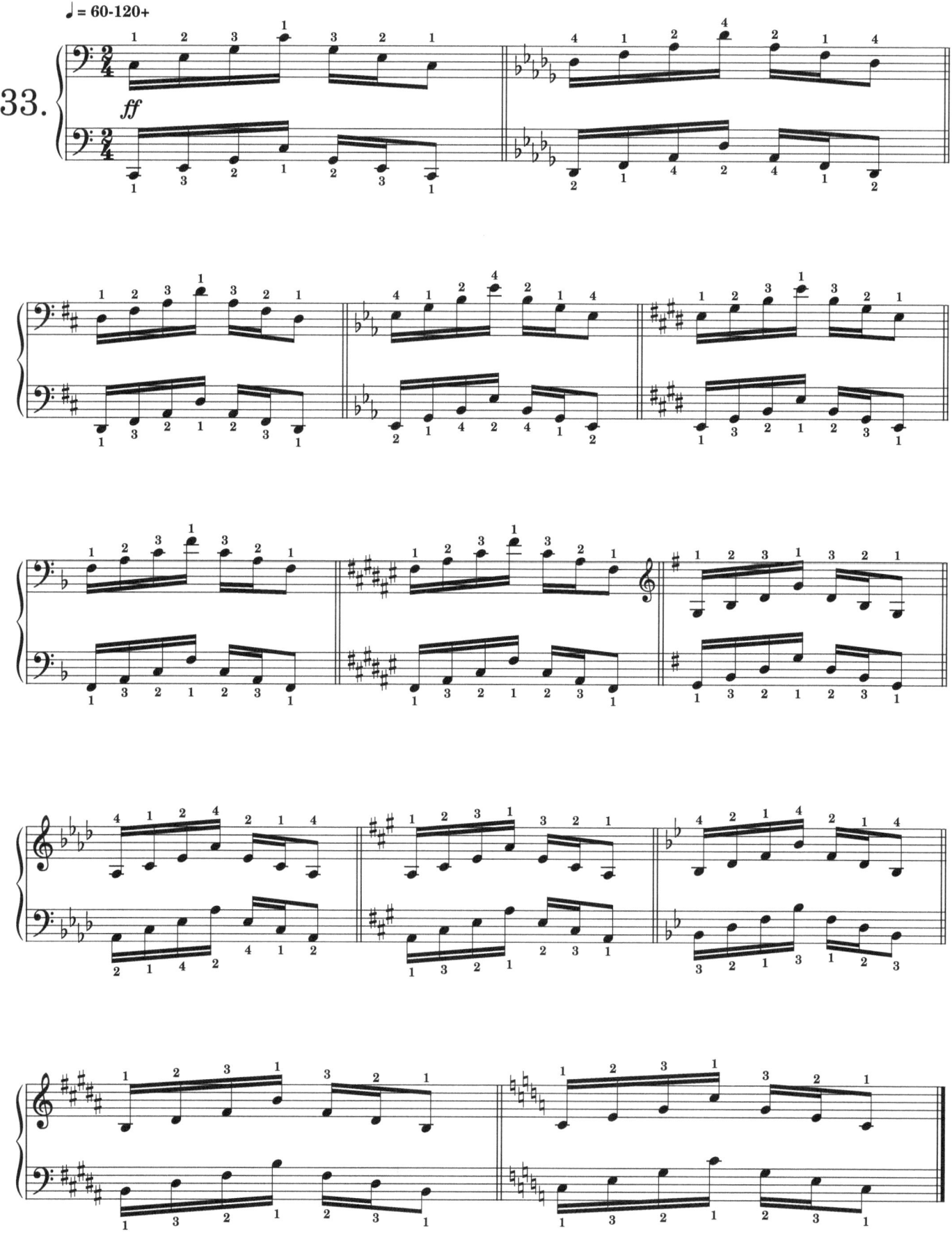

Two-octave major arpeggios. Follow the fingering carefully.

Harmonized octaves: use only fingers 1, 2, and 5 throughout.

— Workout #1 —

Major scales in harmonized octaves. Use only fingers 1, 2, and 5 throughout.

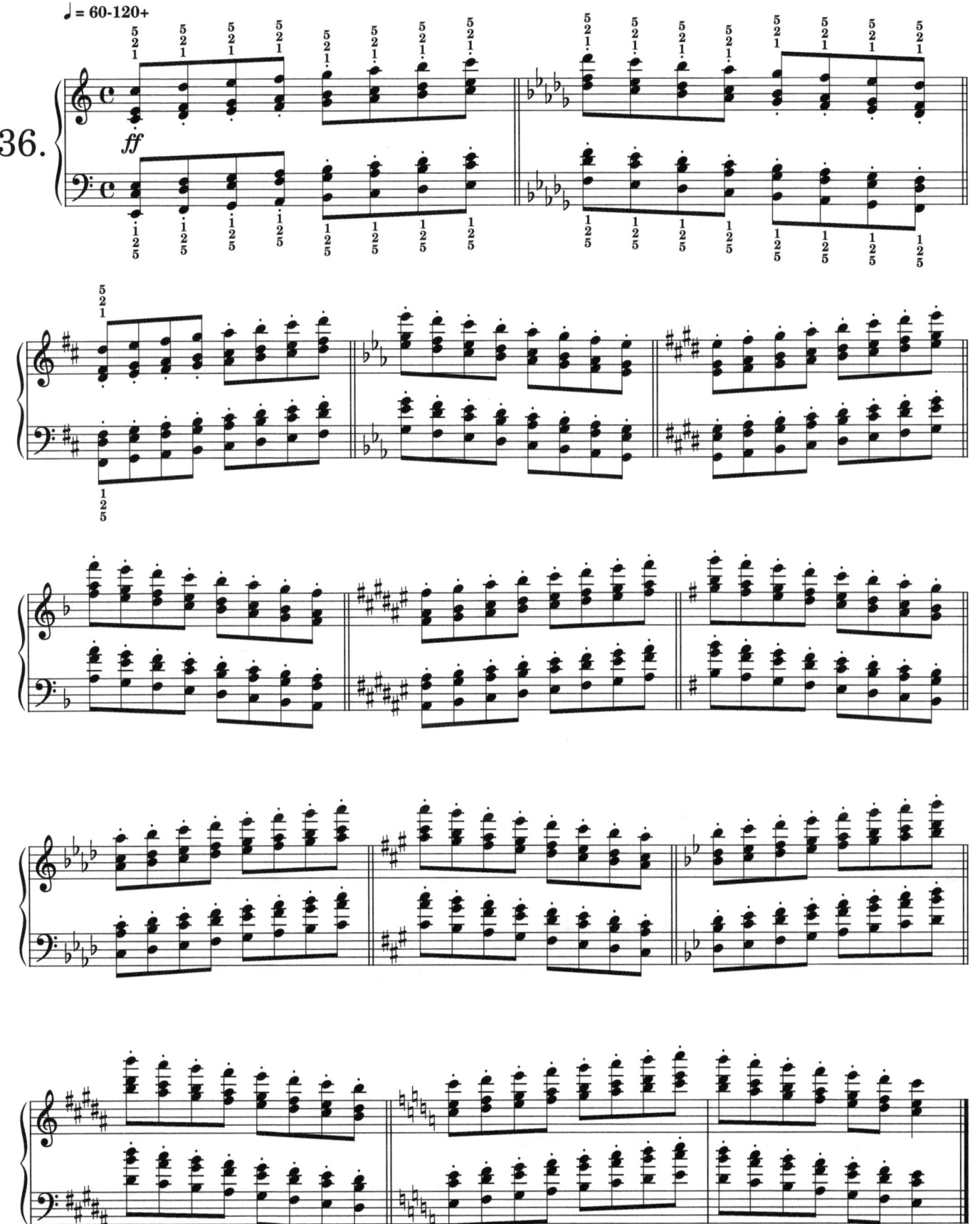

Broken harmonized octaves. Note the different ascending and descending figures.

— Workout #1 —

Dexterity exercise in contrary motion with each hand spanning a 10th.

— Workout #1 —

Dexterity exercise with each hand spanning an 11th and an emphasis on the 4-5 stretch.

— Workout #1 —

Dexterity exercise in contrary motion with each hand spanning a 10th. Play legato throughout.

Workout #2

— Workout #2 —

Dexterity exercise with emphasis on 5-note scale fragments.

— Workout #2 —

Dexterity exercise with emphasis on fingers 3, 4, and 5 in the RH (ascending) and LH (descending).

Dexterity exercise involving broken thirds.

— Workout #2 —

Dexterity exercise beginning with a trill figure.

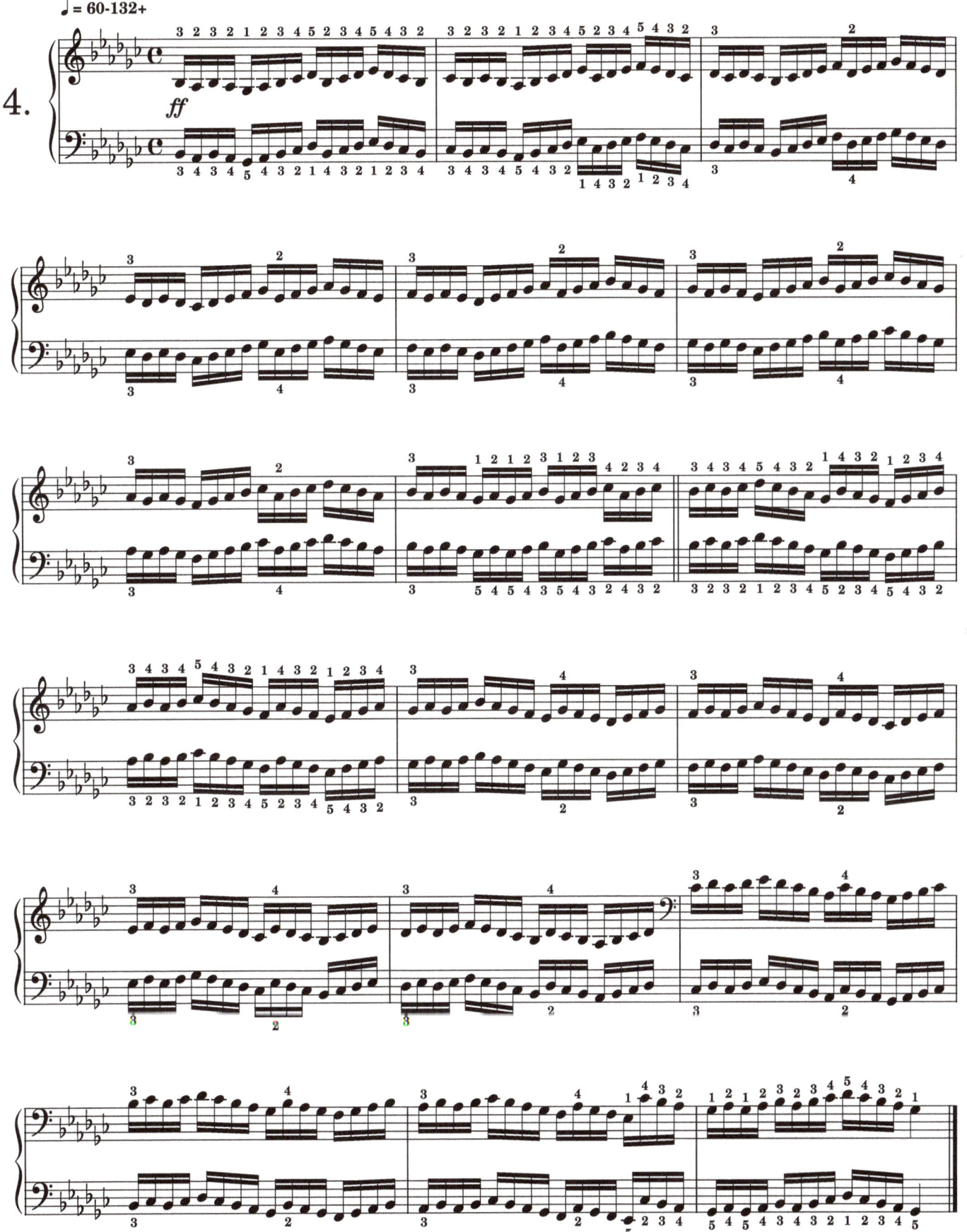

— Workout #2 —

Dexterity exercise with emphasis on 3-4 independence in the LH (ascending) and RH (descending).

Stability exercise: use only the 4th finger of each hand throughout.

6.

— Workout #2 —

Stability exercise: use only the 5th finger of each hand throughout.

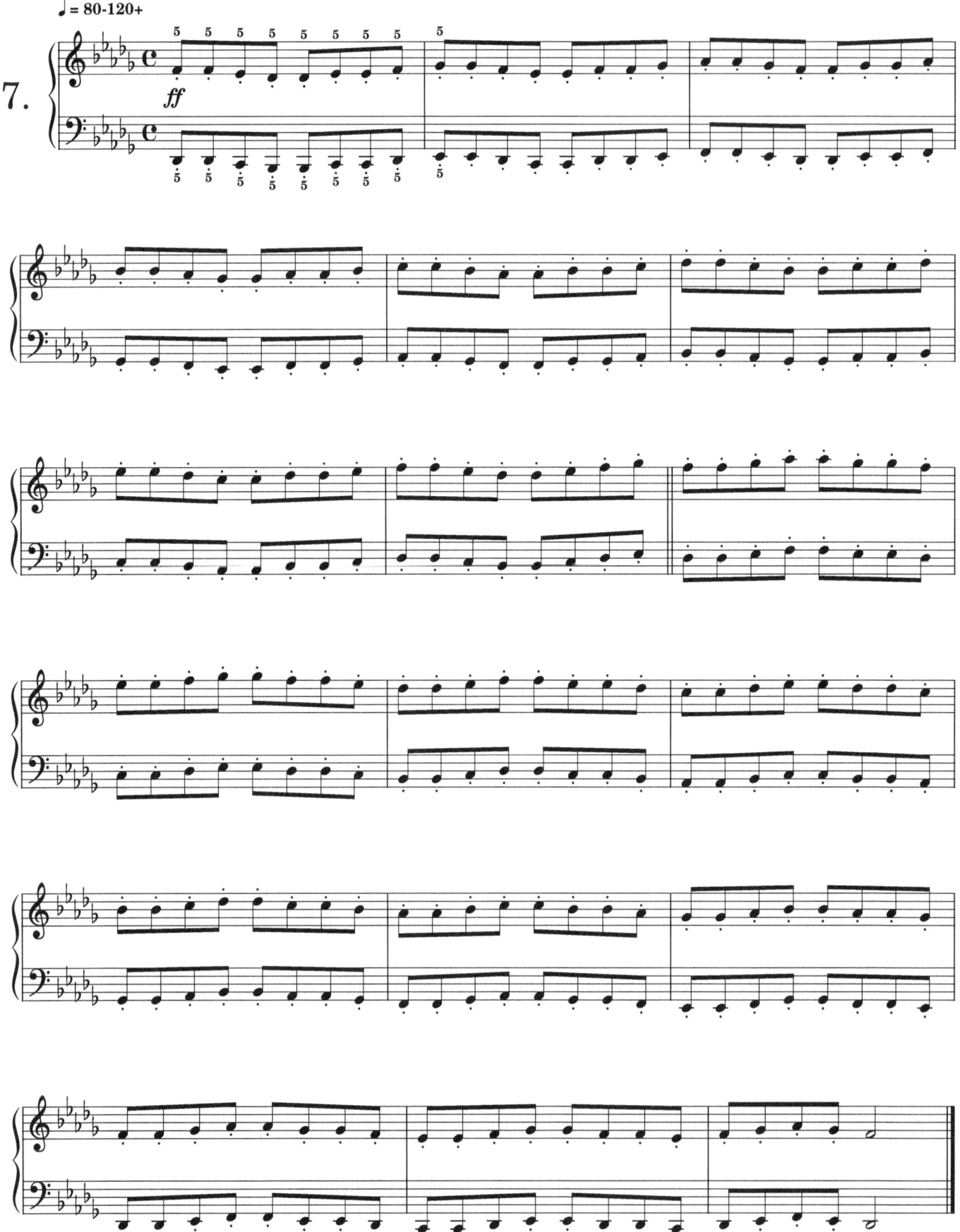

— Workout #2 —

Stability exercise in contrary motion: use only the thumbs throughout.

— Workout #2 —

Exercise for crossing the 4th finger over the thumb.

— Workout #2 —

Exercise for crossing the 5th finger over the thumb. Play all 16th notes legato.

— Workout #2 —

Stability preparation for natural minor scales. Follow the fingering carefully.

— Workout #2 —

Crossover preparation for natural minor scales. Follow the fingering carefully.

— Workout #2 —

One-octave natural minor scales. Follow the fingering carefully.

— Workout #2 —

Two-octave natural minor scales. Follow the fingering carefully.

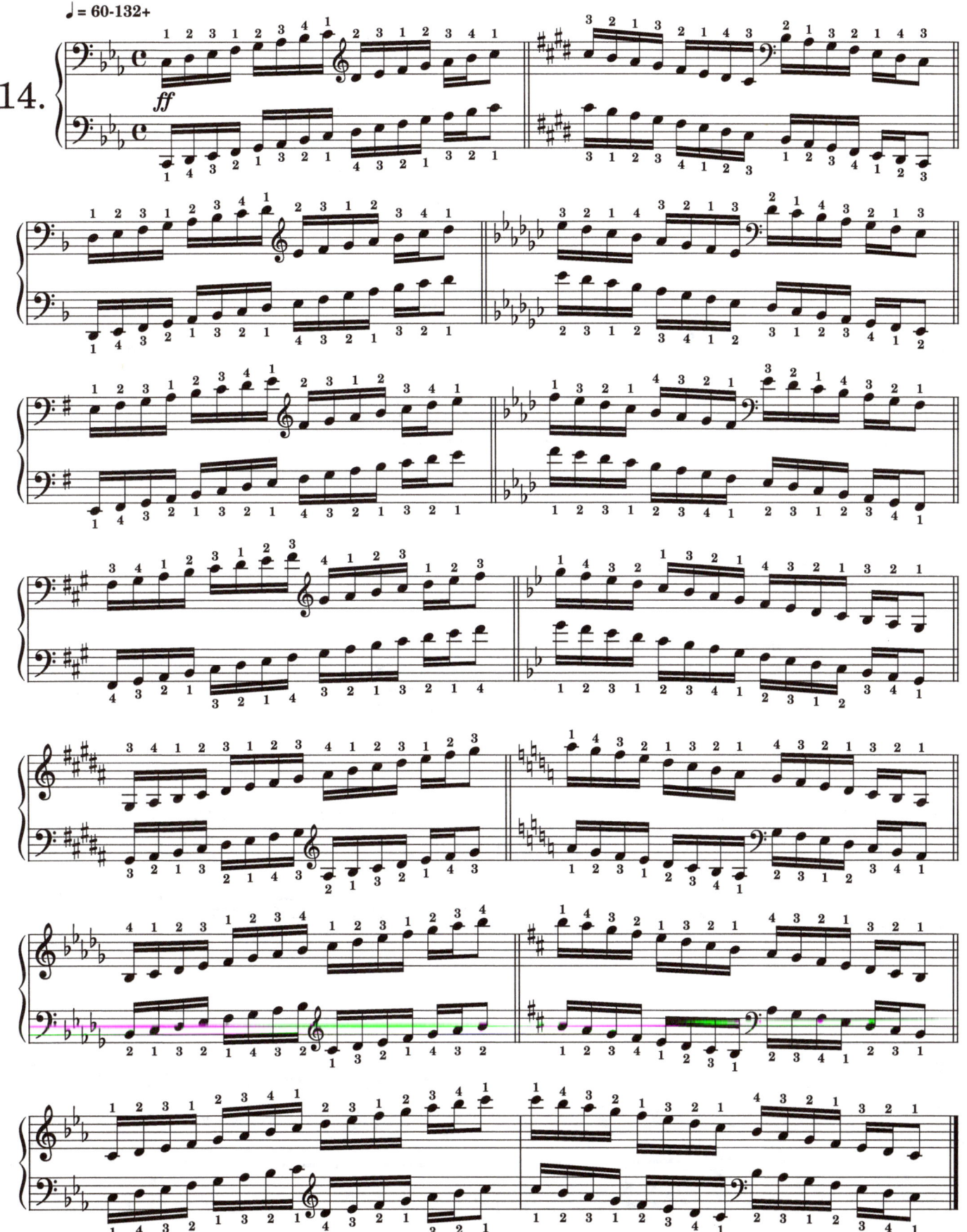

Legato sixths preparation.

— Workout #2 —

Sixths using fingers 3-4-5 in the outer voices. Play as legato as possible.

Workout #2

Sixths using fingers 2-3-4-5 in the outer voices. Play as legato as possible.

— Workout #2 —

Polyphonic exercise with a trill figure in the inner voices.

— Workout #2 —

Dexterity exercise for fingers 3, 4, and 5 while holding down the thumb.

— Workout #2 —

Polyphonic exercise with active inner voices.

— Workout #2 —

Two-note slurs using fingers 2 and 3.

— Workout #2 —

Repeated notes using 3-2-1 and 2-1.

— Workout #2 —

Repeated notes using 4-3-2-1 and 2-1.

— Workout #2 —

Major scales in broken octaves. Use the 4th finger on black keys.

Broken octave stretching exercise. Play legato and use the same fingering pattern throughout.

— Workout #2 —

All harmonic minor scales in broken octaves. Use the 4th finger on black keys.

— Workout #2 —

Dexterity exercise with emphasis on scale fragments.

Workout #2

Dexterity exercise with emphasis on the 3rd finger.

28.

— Workout #2 —

Dexterity exercise targeting a 4-5 stretch in the RH. Play legato throughout.

— Workout #2 —

Dexterity exercise with the hands in close and octave positions.

Stability preparation for minor arpeggios. Follow the fingering carefully.

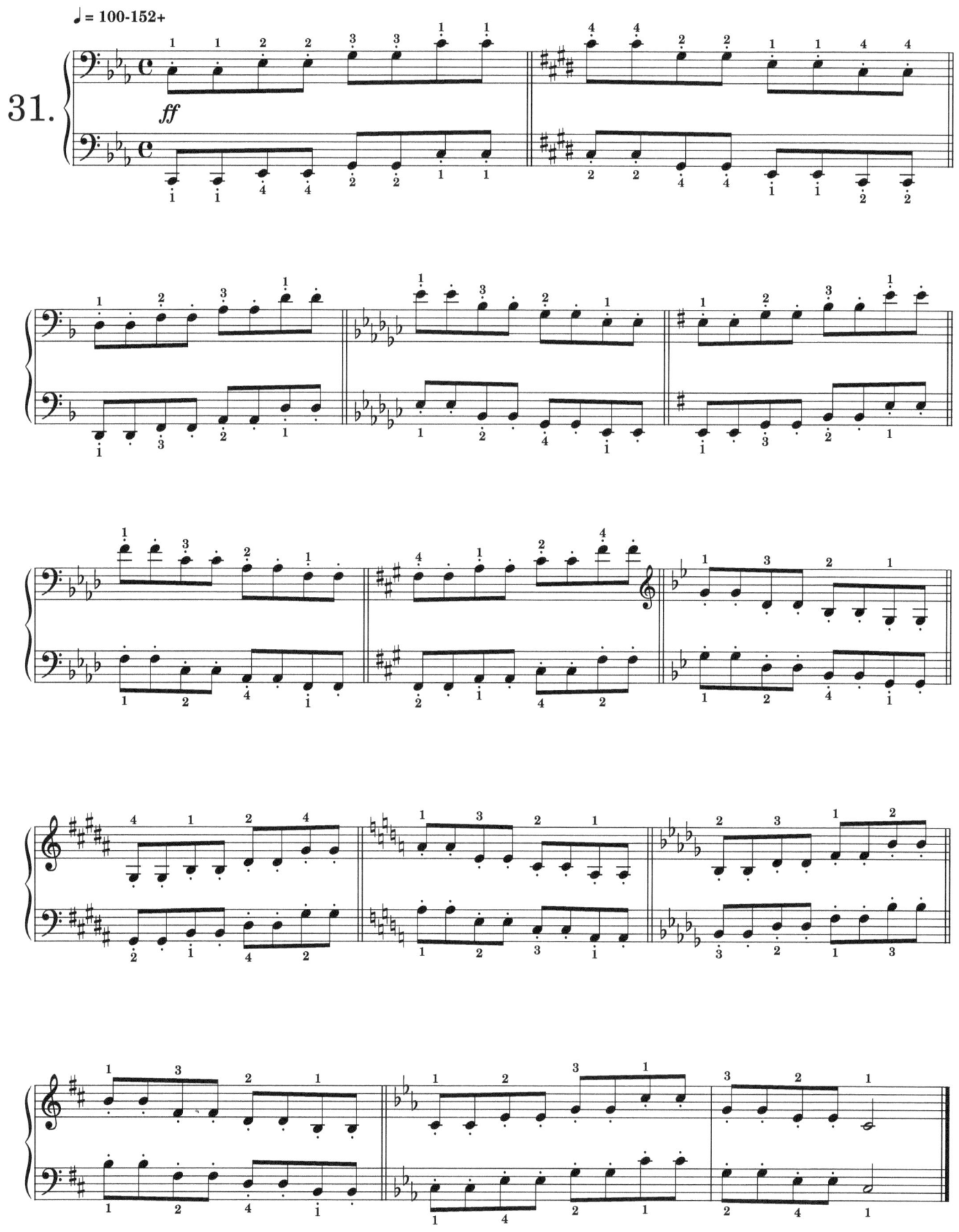

— Workout #2 —

Crossover preparation for minor arpeggios. Follow the fingering carefully.

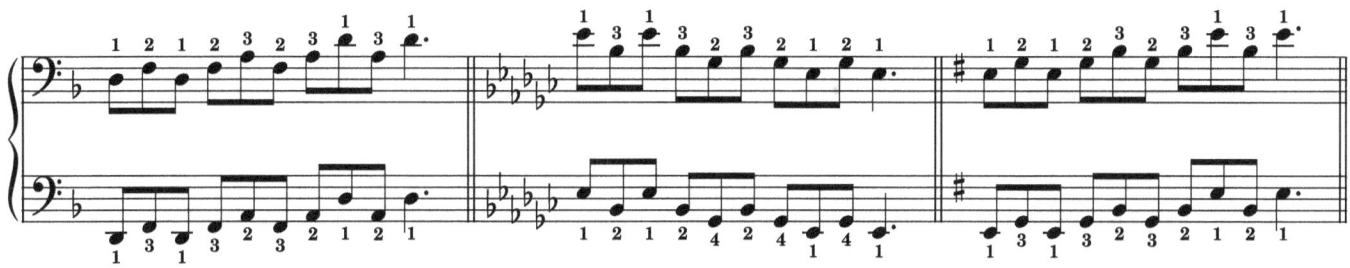

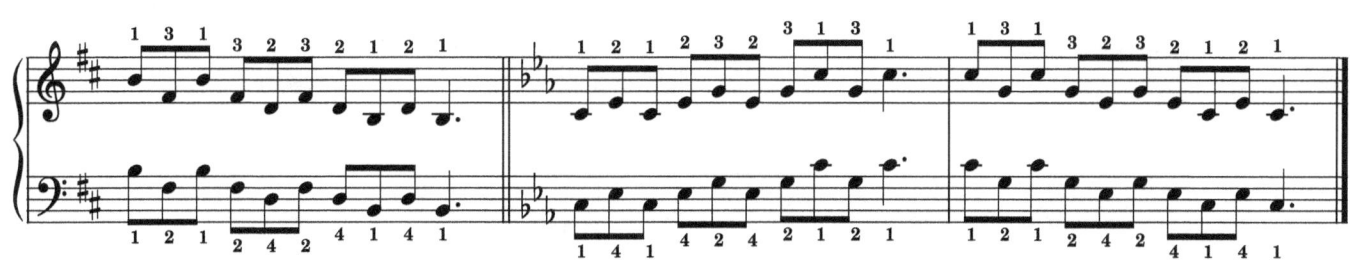

— Workout #2 —

One-octave minor arpeggios. Follow the fingering carefully.

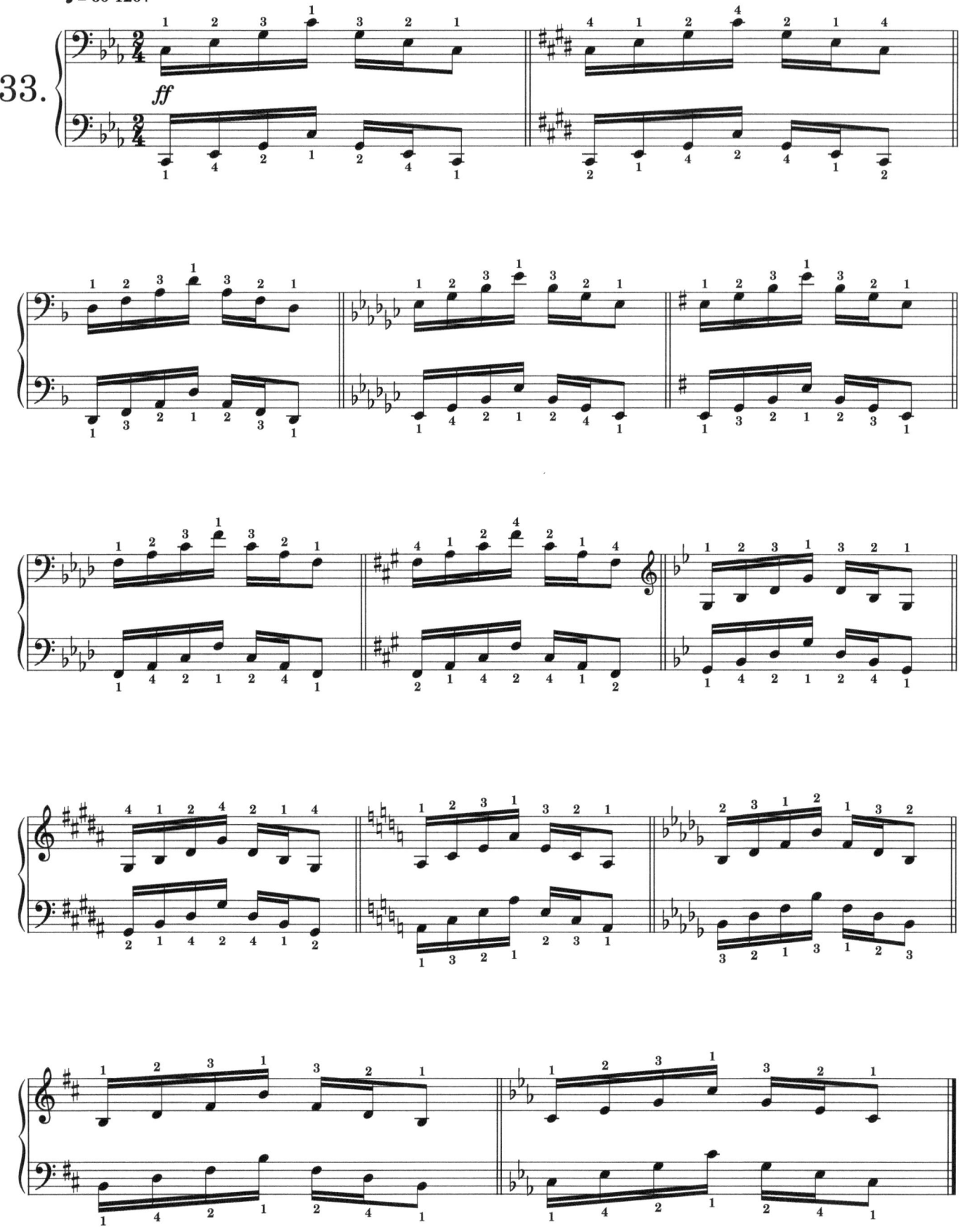

— Workout #2 —

Two-octave minor arpeggios. Follow the fingering carefully.

— Workout #2 —

Four-note major triads in all positions, ascending and descending through the chromatic scale. Use the same fingering for all chords in each position.

— Workout #2 —

Four-note major triads in all keys. Use the same fingering pattern for each key.

— Workout #2 —

Broken 4-note triads. Use the same fingering throughout each position (root position, 1st inversion, 2nd inversion).

— Workout #2 —

Dexterity exercise with each hand spanning a 10th. Play legato throughout, including from measure to measure.

— Workout #2 —

Dexterity exercise with each hand spanning a 12th.

— Workout #2 —

Dexterity exercise in contrary motion with the RH spanning an 11th and the LH spanning a 10th. Play all 16th notes legato.

Workout #3

— Workout #3 —

Dexterity exercise with emphasis on scale fragments and broken thirds.

— Workout #3 —

Dexterity exercise with emphasis on fingers 2, 3, and 4.

— Workout #3 —

Dexterity exercise with frequent changes of direction.

— Workout #3 —

Dexterity exercise with emphasis on 4-5 in the RH (ascending) and LH (descending).

— Workout #3 —

Dexterity exercise. Pay close attention to the fingering.

— Workout #3 —

Stability exercise: use only fingers 2 and 5 throughout.

— Workout #3 —

Stability exercise: use only fingers 1 and 5 throughout.

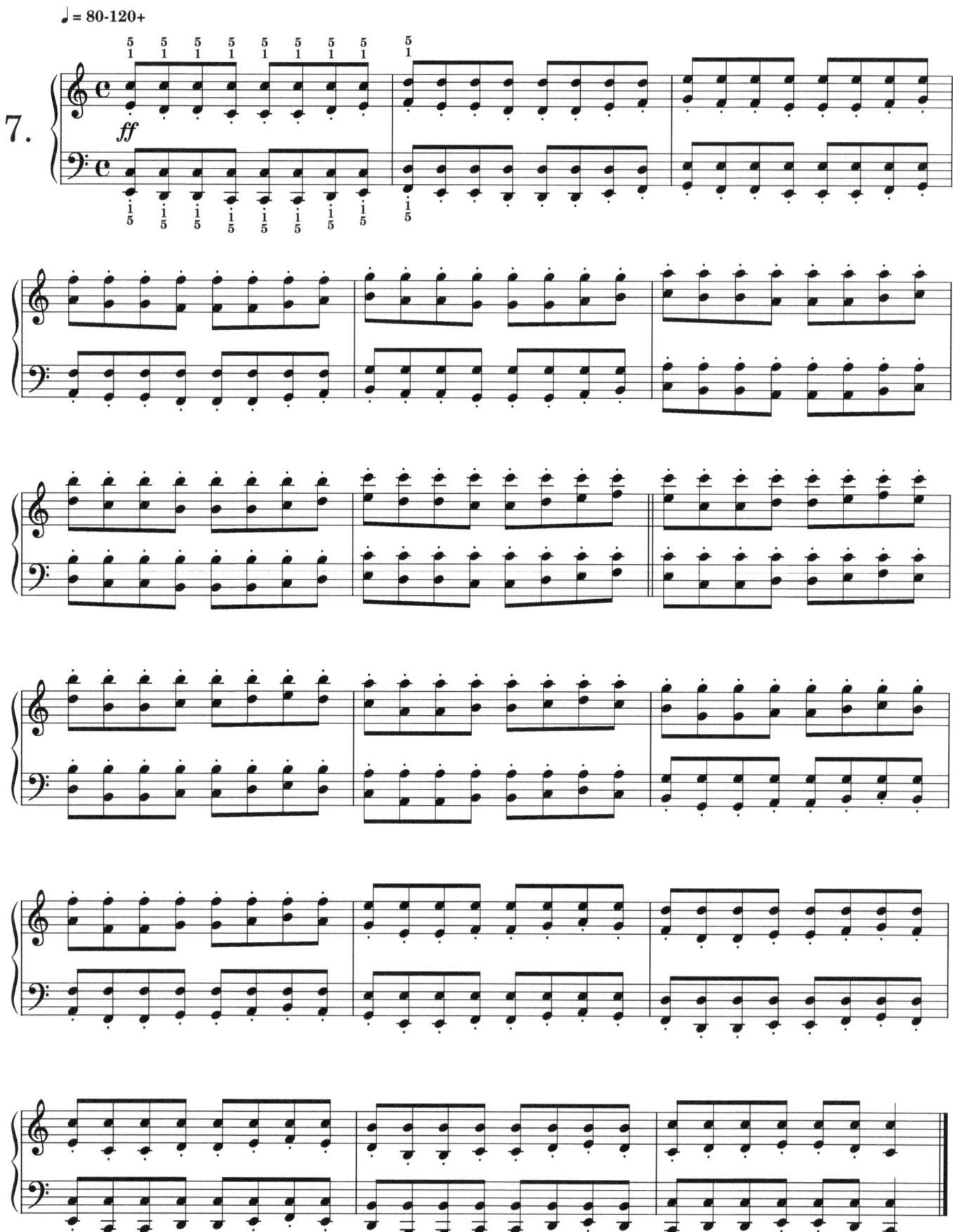

— Workout #3 —

Stability exercise: use only fingers 2 and 4 throughout.

8.

♩ = 80-120+

ff

— Workout #3 —

Exercise for crossing the 2nd finger over the thumb.

94

— Workout #3 —

Exercise for passing the thumb under the 3rd finger.

95

Stability preparation for the chromatic scale.

— Workout #3 —

One-octave chromatic scales.

— Workout #3 —

One-octave chromatic scales with the hands separated by a minor 3rd.

— Workout #3 —

The chromatic scale in contrary motion.

Workout #3

Thirds, with an emphasis on 2-4.

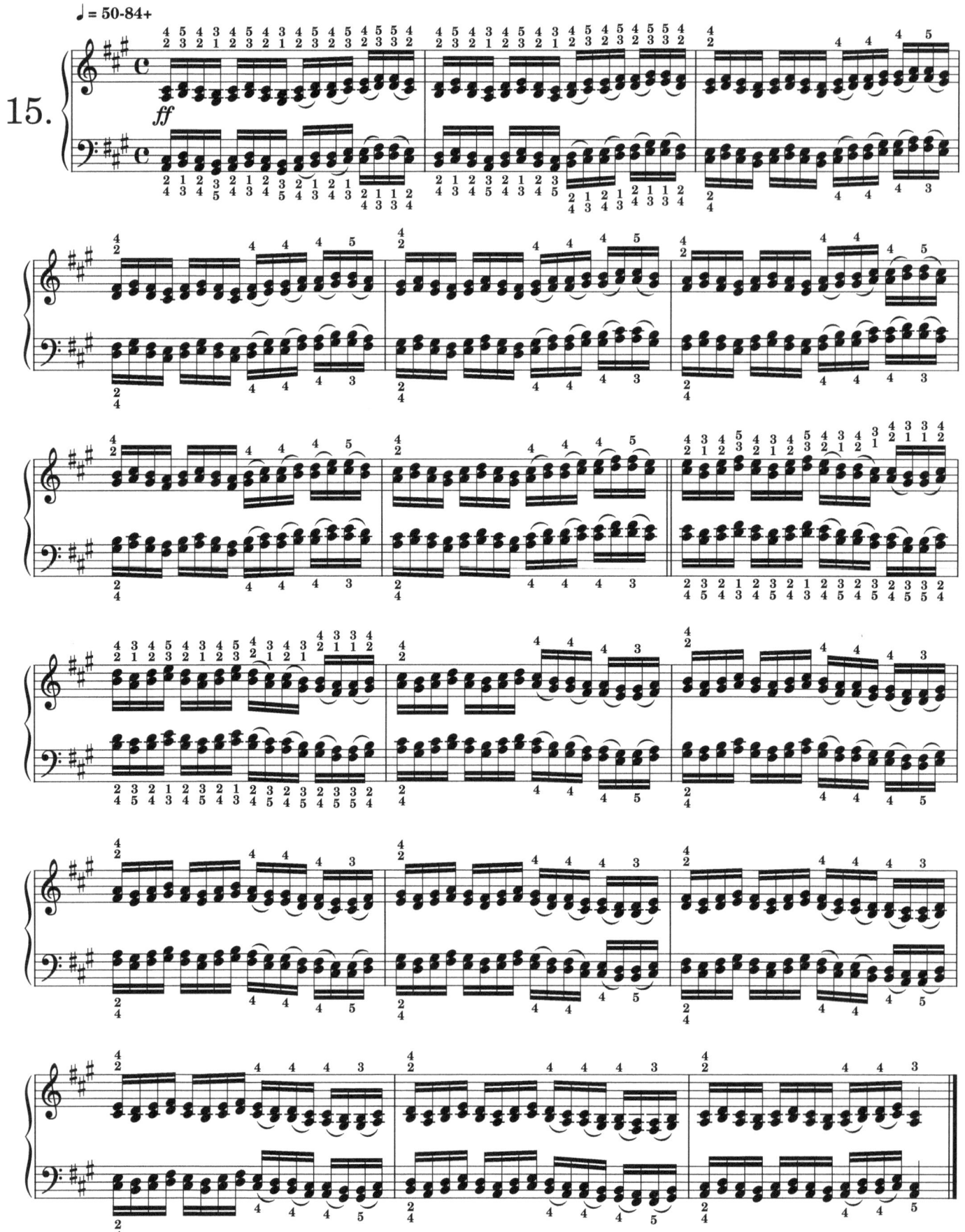

— Workout #3 —

Thirds, using 3-4-5 in the outer voices. Play all 16th notes legato.

— Workout #3 —

Preparation for scales in thirds. Use the same fingering pattern in all keys, and play as legato as possible.

— Workout #3 —

Major scales in thirds. Use the same fingering pattern for each scale, and play as legato as possible.

18.

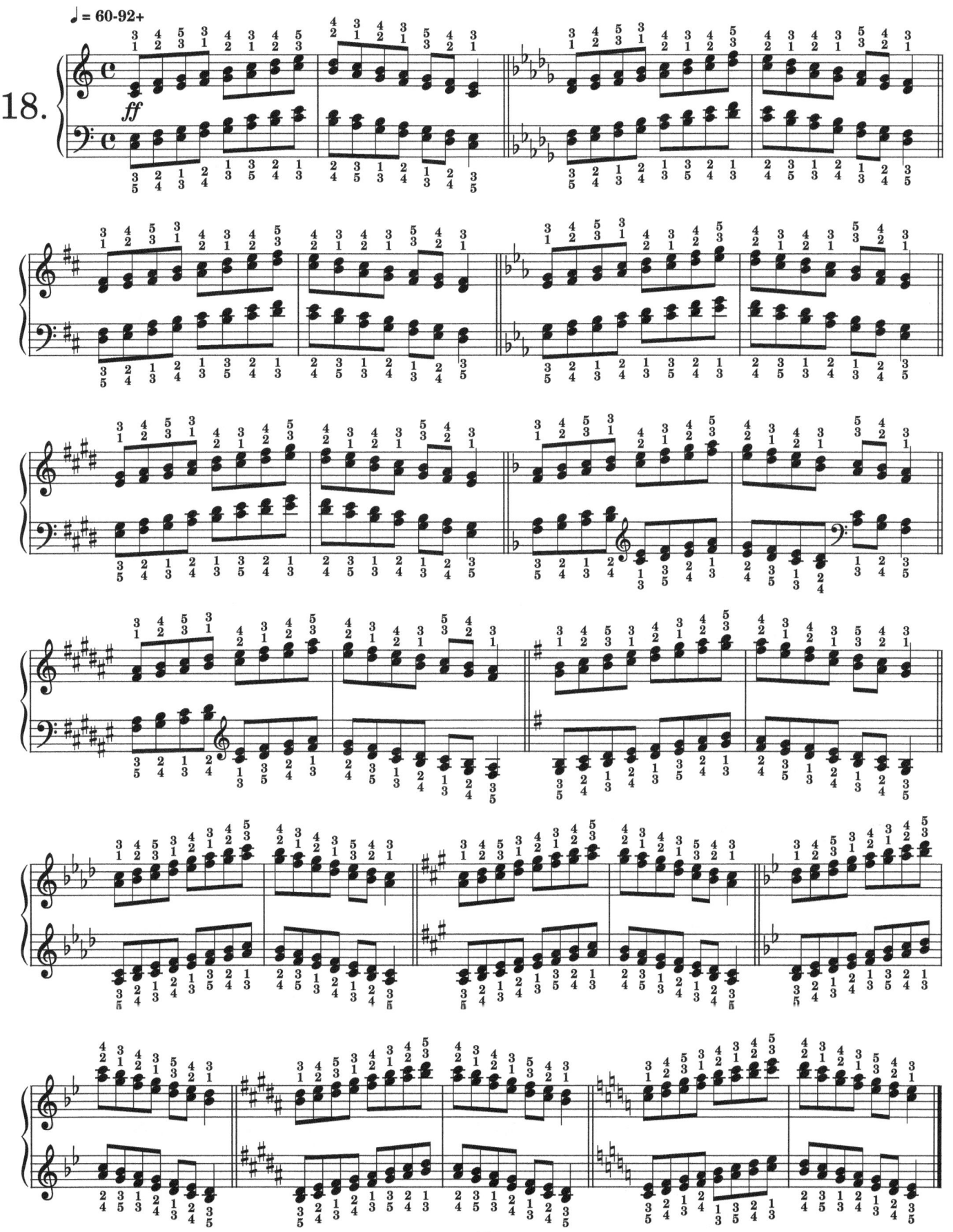

— Workout #3 —

Broken 4-note minor triads in root position, 1st inversion, and 2nd inversion.

— Workout #3 —

Broken 4-note minor triads. Each measure contains root position, 1st inversion, and 2nd inversion.

105

— Workout #3 —

Trill with Nachschlag. Ensure the LH keeps pace with the RH.

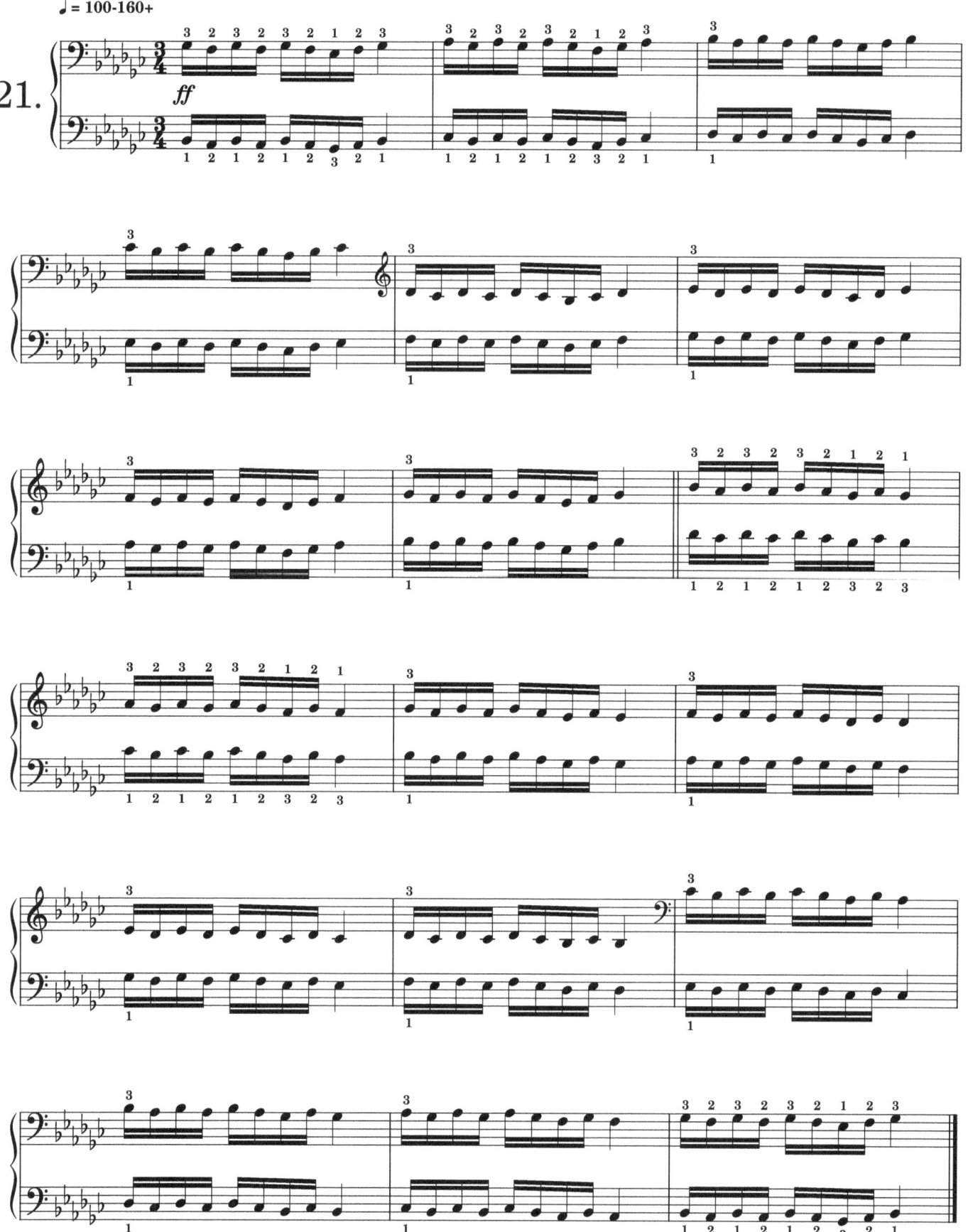

Embellished thirds.

— Workout #3 —

Trills for polyphonic music. RH uses 3-5 for speed and clarity.

— Workout #3 —

The chromatic scale in octaves. Use the 4th finger on black keys.

— Workout #3 —

Chromatic scales in octaves, with hands separated by a minor 10th. Use the 4th finger on black keys.

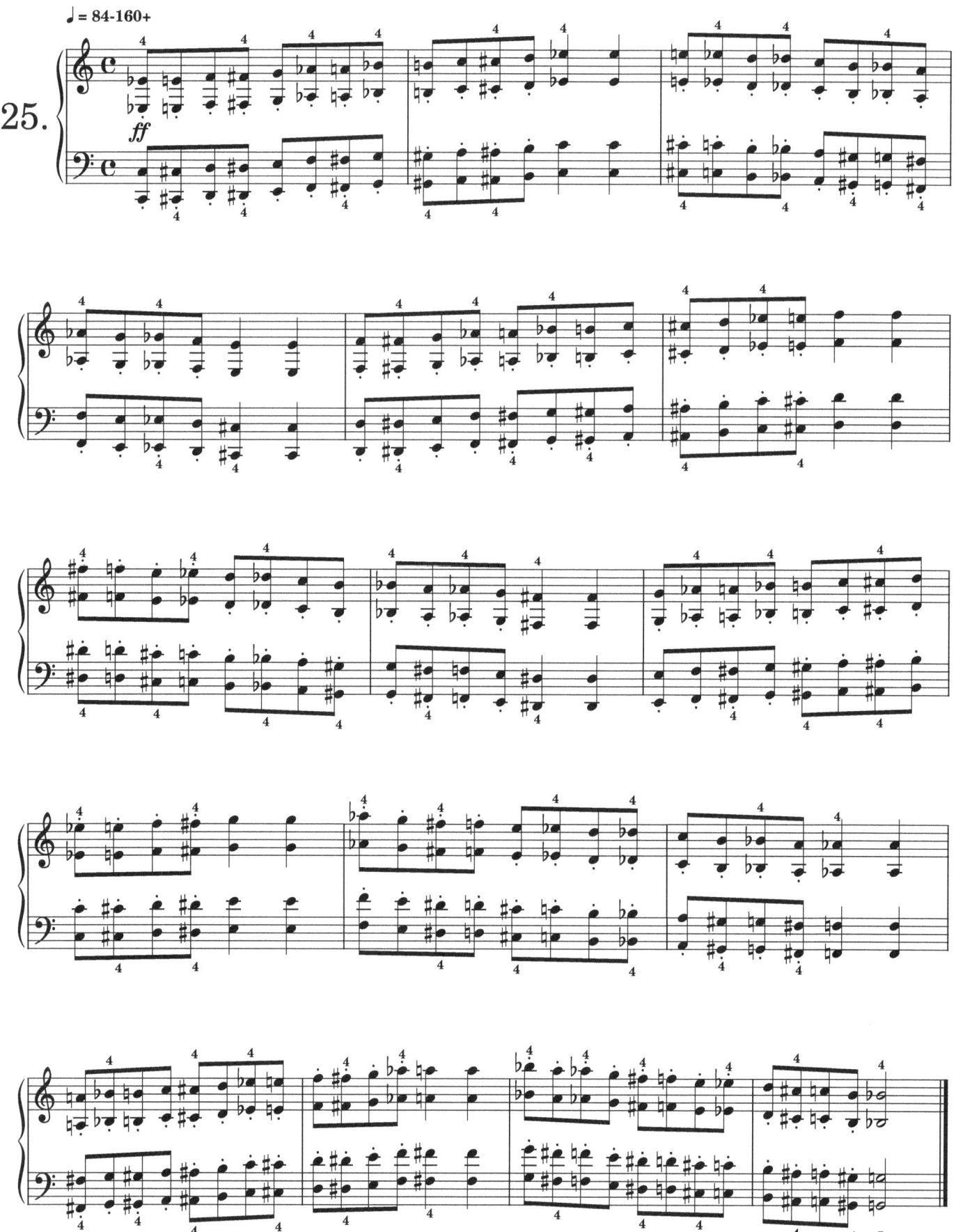

— Workout #3 —

Interlocking chromatic octaves. Use the 4th finger on black keys.

— Workout #3 —

Dexterity exercise using both open and close positions.

— Workout #3 —

Dexterity exercise with emphasis on the 3rd finger. Play legato, including from measure to measure.

— Workout #3 —

Dexterity exercise with emphasis on broken thirds.

— Workout #3 —

Dexterity exercise with increasing 3-5 stretches in the RH (ascending) and LH (descending).

— Workout #3 —

Stability preparation for dominant 7th arpeggios. Follow the fingering carefully. (Key signatures match the root of the chord.)

— Workout #3 —

Crossover preparation for dominant 7th arpeggios. Follow the fingering carefully.

♩ = 80-120+

32.

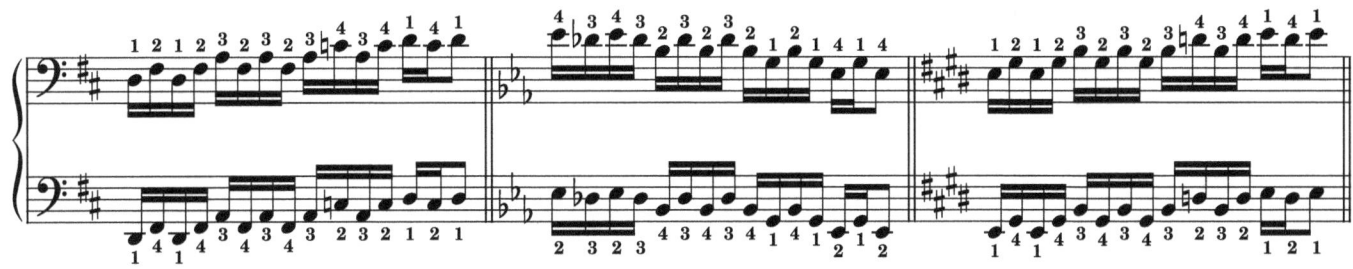

— Workout #3 —

One-octave dominant 7th arpeggios. Follow the fingering carefully.

Two-octave dominant 7th arpeggios. Follow the fingering carefully.

— Workout #3 —

Stability preparation for harmonized octaves. Use fingers 1, 3, and 5 throughout.

— Workout #3 —

All major scales in harmonized octaves. Use fingers 1, 3, and 5 throughout.

— Workout #3 —

Broken harmonized octaves. Note the different ascending and descending figures.

— Workout #3 —

Dexterity exercise in contrary motion with the RH spanning a 10th and the LH a 12th.

— Workout #3 —

Common broken chord voicing, spanning a 10th.

— Workout #3 —

Dexterity exercise spanning a 12th in each hand.

40.

♩ = 60-120+

ff

Workout #4

— Workout #4 —

Dexterity exercise with emphasis on the thumb and 5th finger.

— Workout #4 —

Dexterity exercise involving scale fragments and contraction of the hand.

— Workout #4 —

Dexterity exercise involving a neighbor tones.

— Workout #4 —

Dexterity exercise with an alternation pattern.

— Workout #4 —

Dexterity exercise with scale fragments and changes of direction.

— Workout #4 —

Stability exercise: use only fingers 2 and 5 throughout.

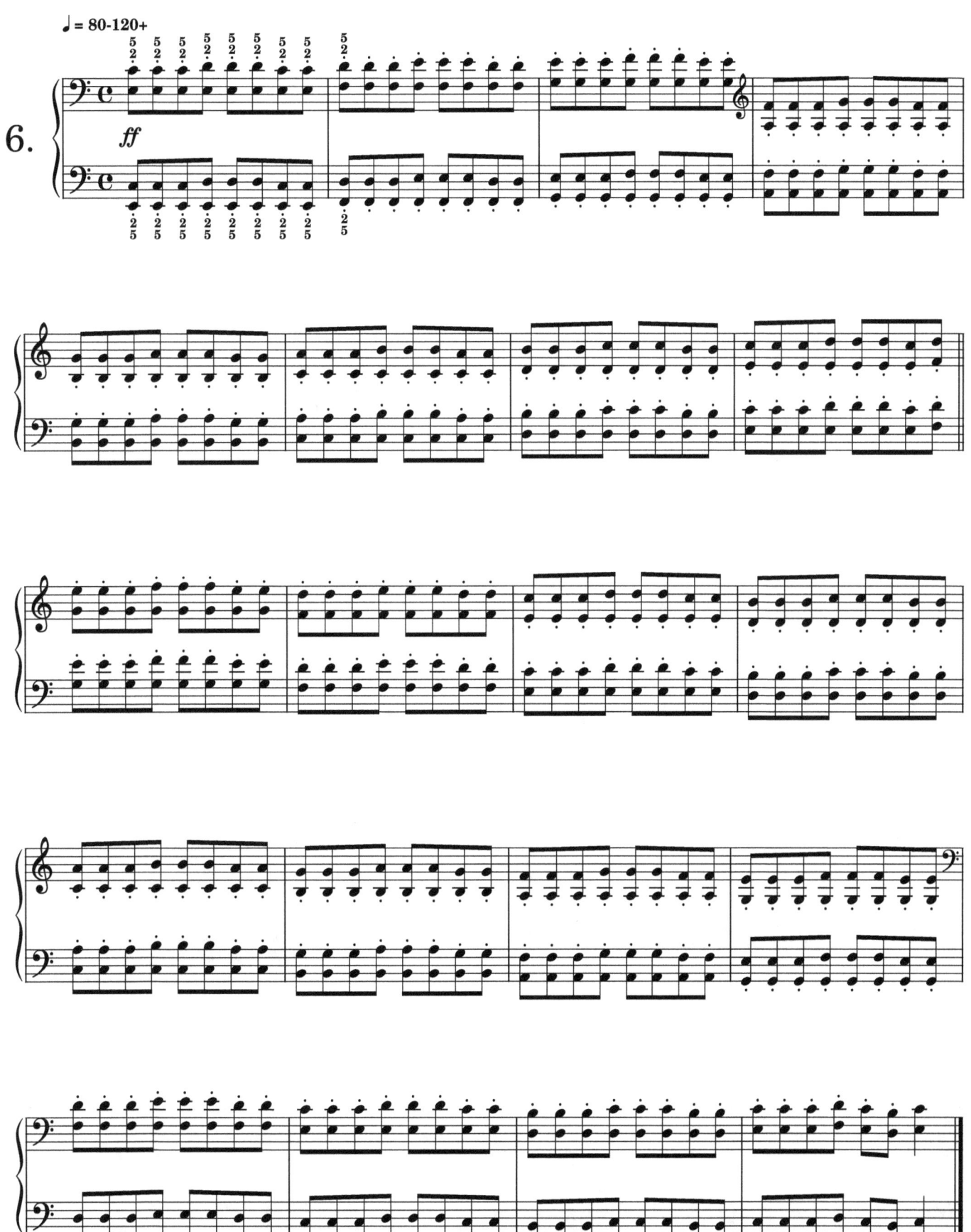

— Workout #4 —

Stability exercise: use only fingers 3 and 5 throughout.

— Workout #4 —

Stability exercise: use only fingers 4 and 5 throughout.

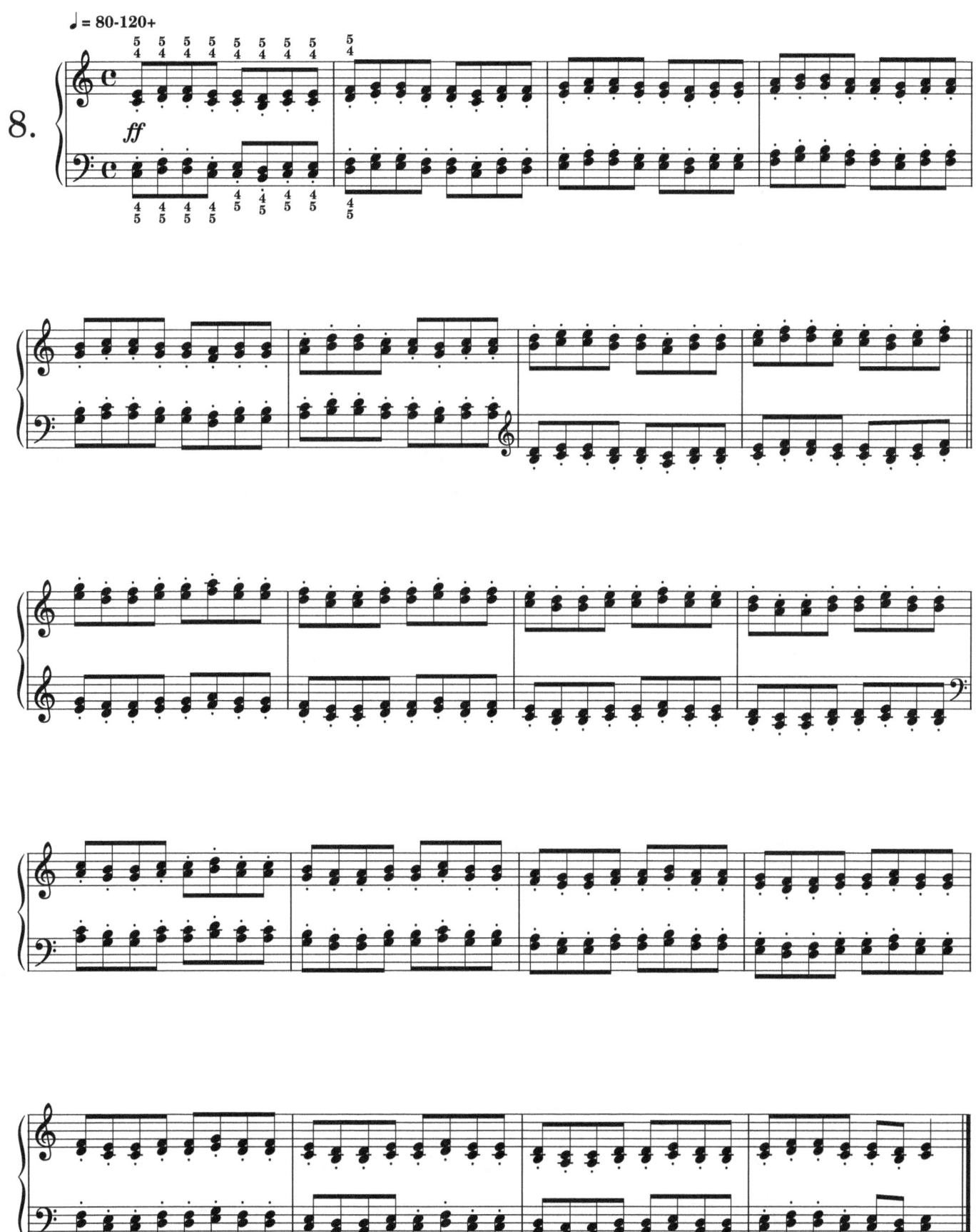

— Workout #4 —

Exercise for positioning the thumb under the hand.

— Workout #4 —

Exercise in contrary motion for positioning the thumb under the hand.

— Workout #4 —

Stability preparation for harmonic minor scales. Follow the fingering carefully.

— Workout #4 —

Crossover preparation for harmonic minor scales. Follow the fingering carefully.

— Workout #4 —

One-octave harmonic minor scales. Follow the fingering carefully.

— Workout #4 —

Two-octave harmonic minor scales. Follow the fingering carefully.

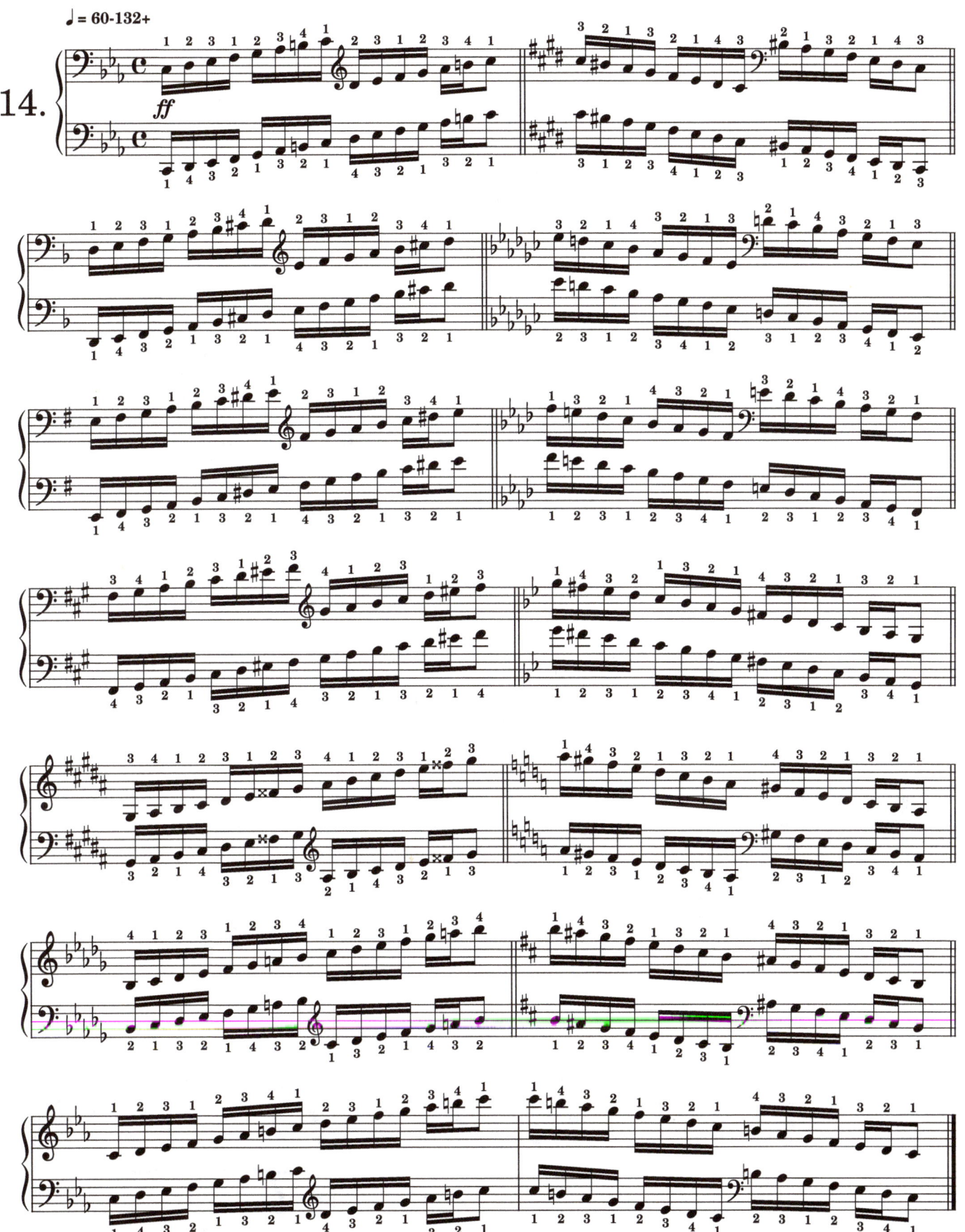

— Workout #4 —

Preparation for scales in sixths. Play as legato as possible.

— Workout #4 —

Major scales in sixths. Use 14-25 throughout and play as legato as possible.

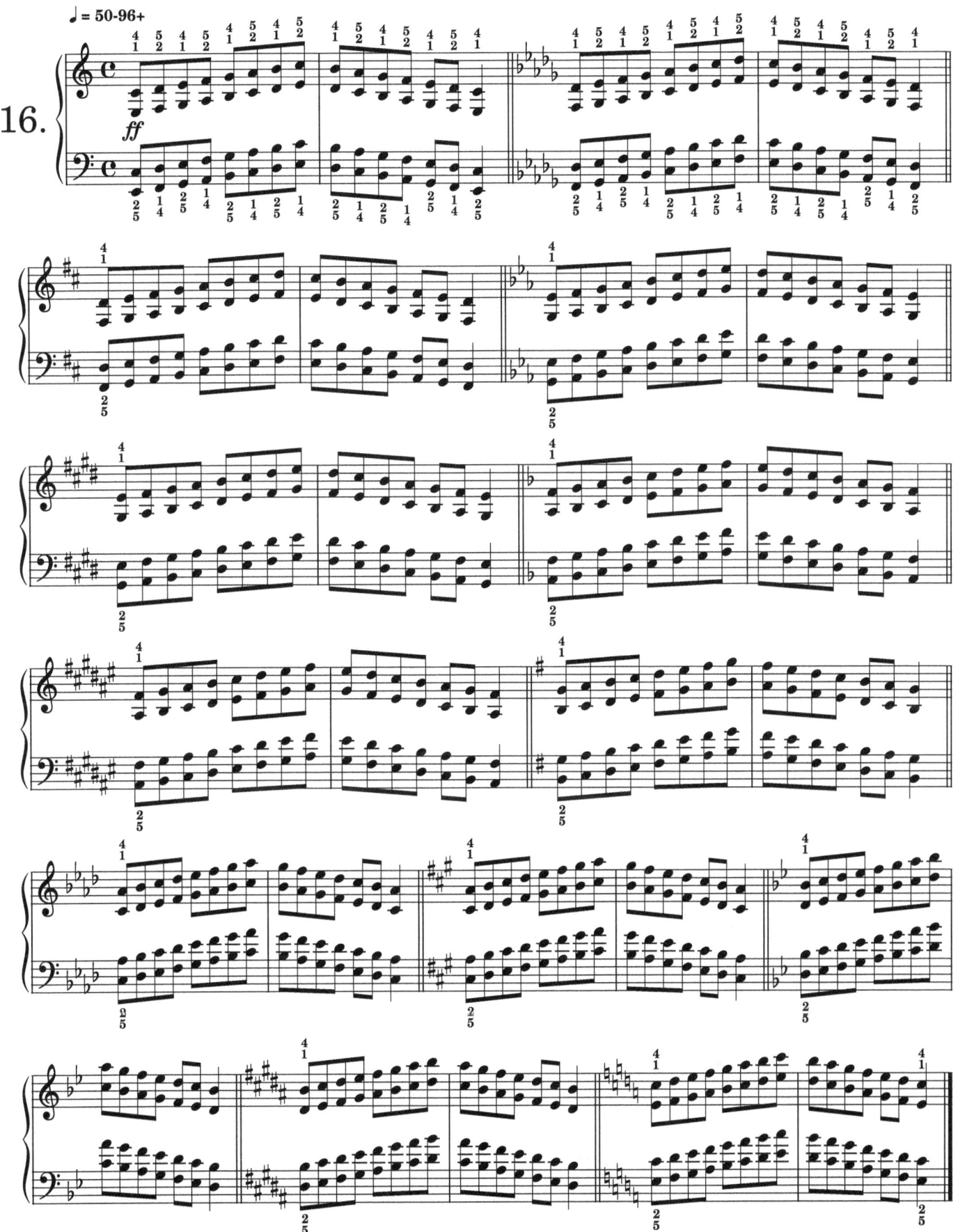

— Workout #4 —

Chromatic minor sixths. Use 14-25 throughout.

— Workout #4 —

Five-note broken minor 7th chords.

— Workout #4 —

Five-note broken half-diminished 7th chords. (Key signatures match the root of the chord.)

146

Legato octaves using 1-4 and 1-5.

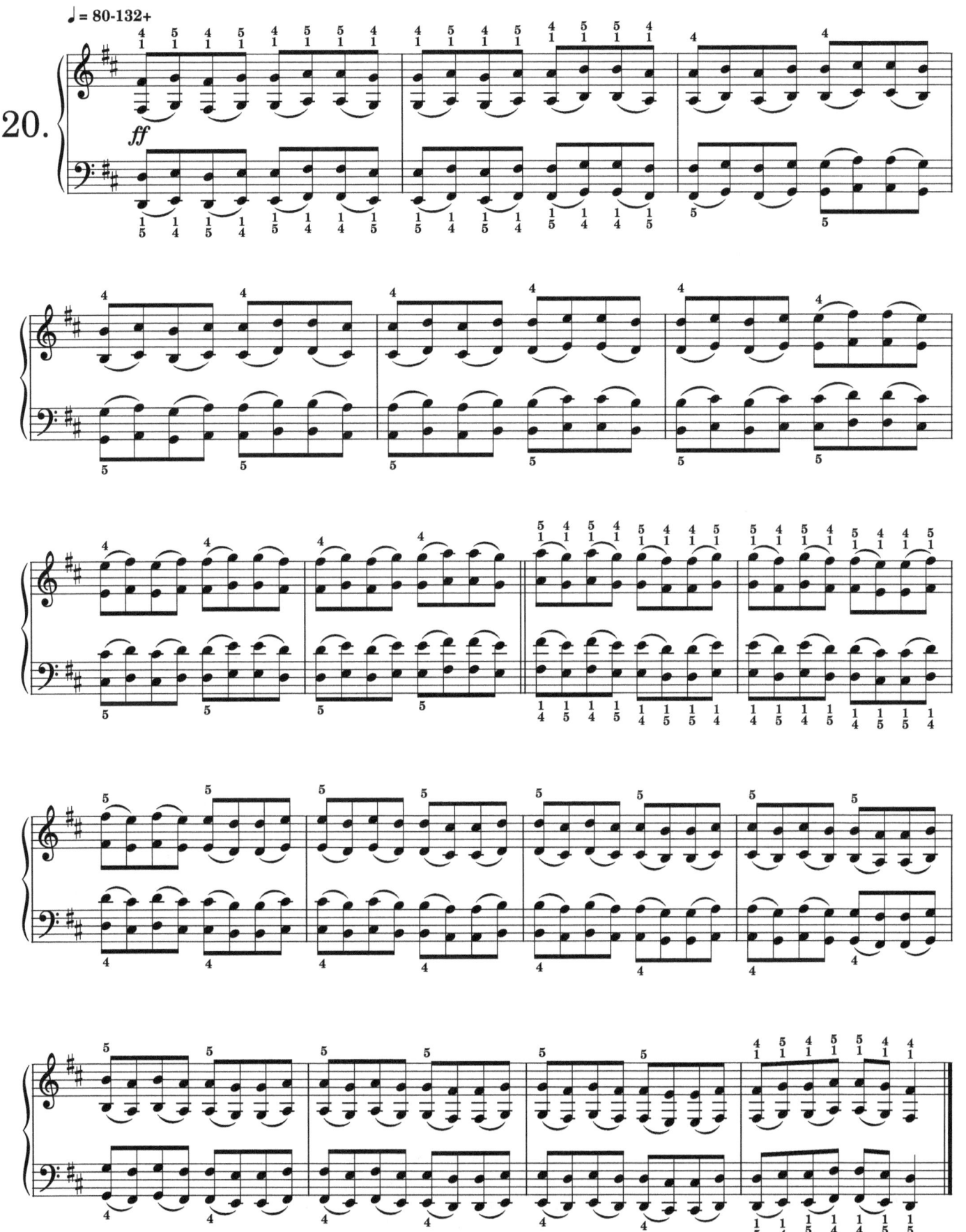

— Workout #4 —

Octaves using 1-3, 1-4, and 1-5. Play the outer voices legato.

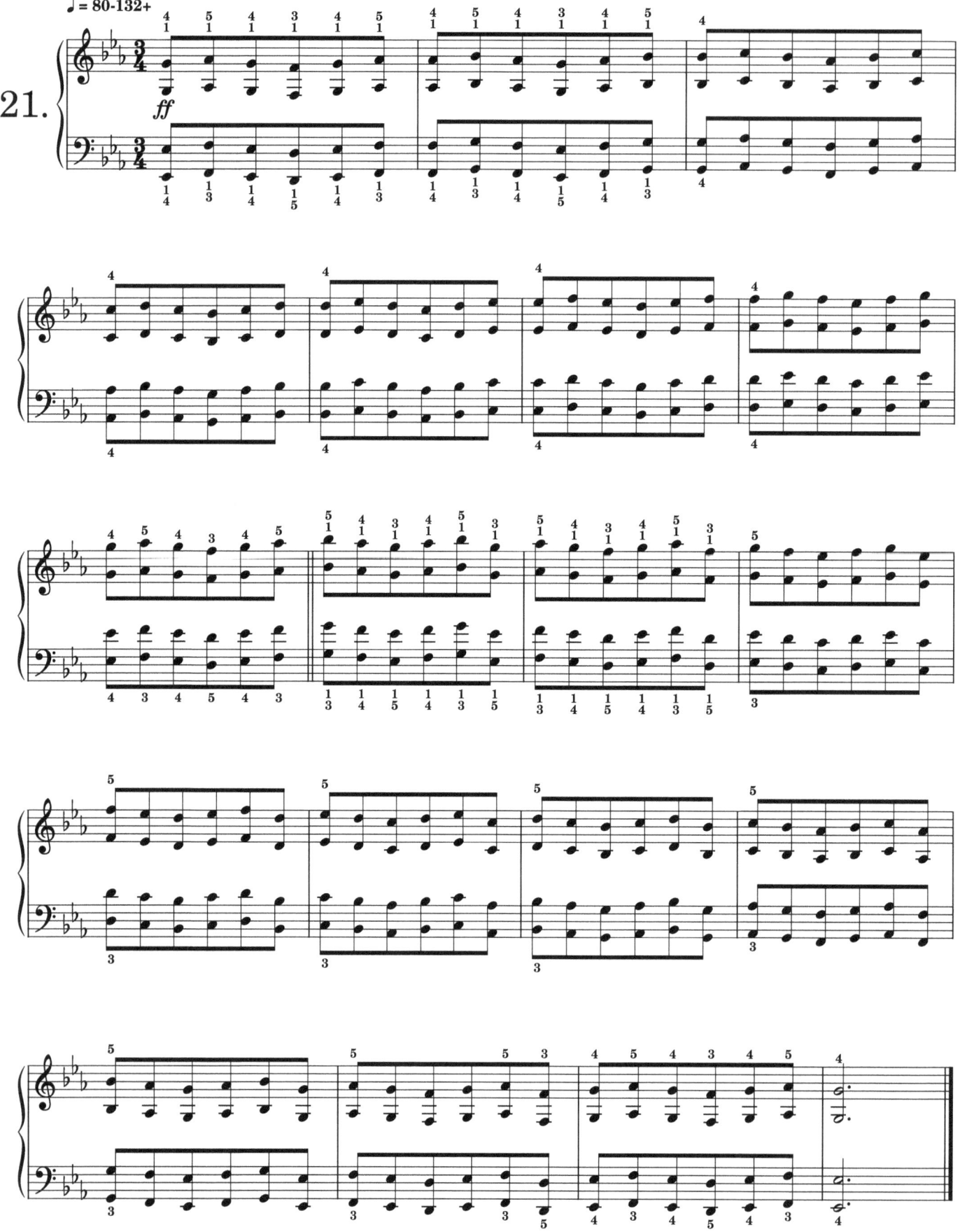

Octave pattern using 1-3, 1-4, and 1-5. Play the 8th notes as legato as possible.

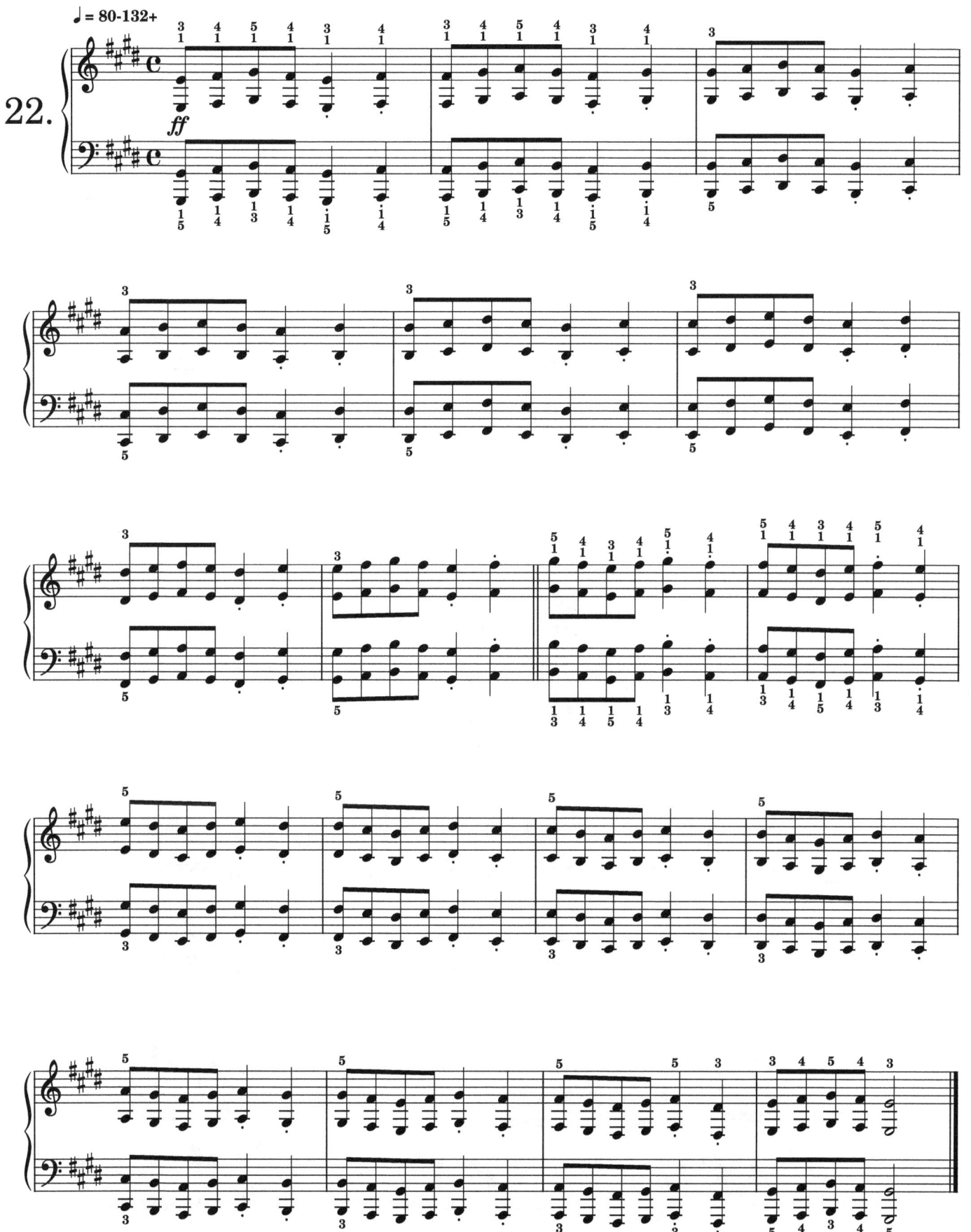

— Workout #4 —

Broken-chord figure with single and double notes.

23. ♪ = 120-180+

Another broken-chord figure with single and double notes.

— Workout #4 —

Horn fifths in contrary motion.

— Workout #4 —

Broken major triads in double notes. Use the same fingering pattern in each key.

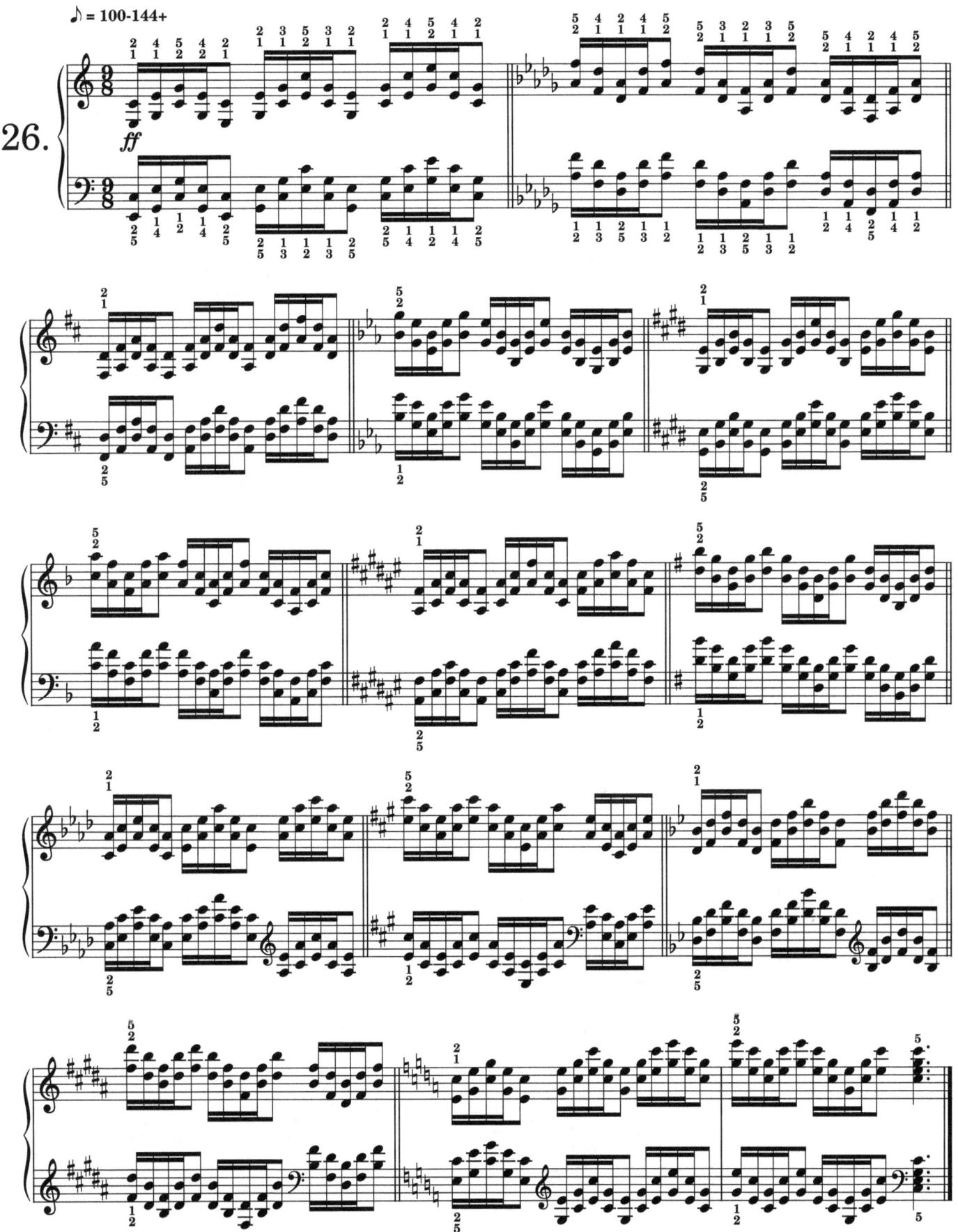

— Workout #4 —

Dexterity exercise with quick crossovers and thumb passes.

— Workout #4 —

Dexterity exercise with quick stretches.

— Workout #4 —

Dexterity exercise involving 2-4 contraction.

— Workout #4 —

Dexterity exercise with an alternation pattern.

— Workout #4 —

Stability preparation for diminished 7th arpeggios. Follow the fingering carefully.

— Workout #4 —

Crossover preparation for diminished 7th arpeggios. Follow the fingering carefully.

— Workout #4 —

One-octave diminished 7th arpeggios. Follow the fingering carefully.

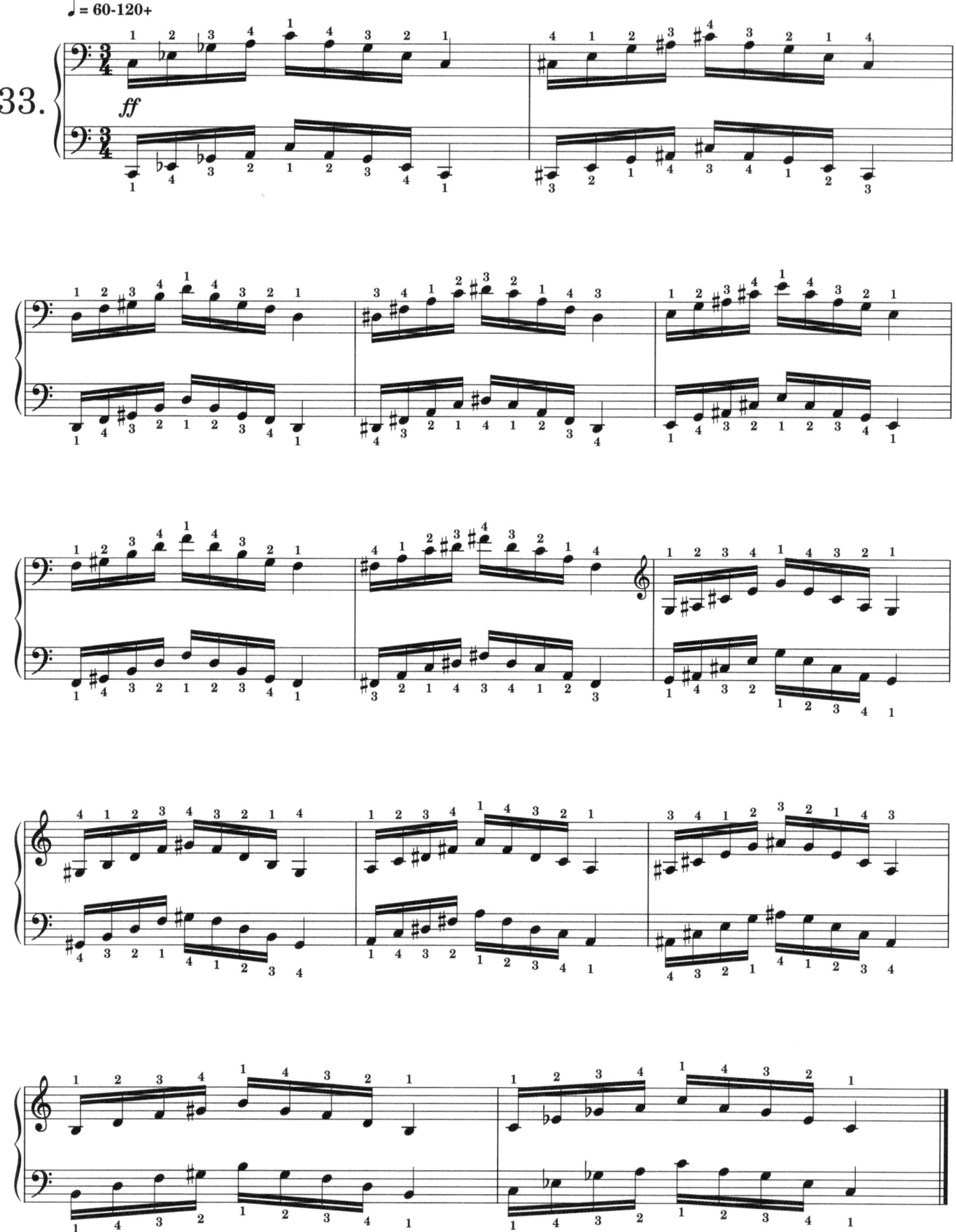

— Workout #4 —

Two-octave diminished 7th arpeggios. Follow the fingering carefully.

— Workout #4 —

Four-note minor triads in all positions, ascending and descending through the chromatic scale. Use the same fingering for all chords in each position.

— Workout #4 —

Four-note minor triads in root position, 1st inversion, and 2nd inversion. Use the same fingering pattern for each key.

Broken 4-note triads in C minor. Use the same fingering throughout each position (root position, 1st inversion, 2nd inversion).

— Workout #4 —

Dexterity exercise in contrary motion with the RH spanning an 11th and LH a 10th. Emphasis on the 3-5 stretch.

— Workout #4 —

Dexterity exercise with each hand spanning a 10th.

— Workout #4 —

Dexterity exercise in contrary motion with each hand spanning a 12th.

167

Workout #5

— Workout #5 —

Dexterity exercise emphasizing scale fragments and changes of direction.

— Workout #5 —

Dexterity exercise with emphasis on the 4th finger in the RH (ascending) and LH (descending).

— Workout #5 —

Dexterity exercise with a quick stretch to the 4th finger in the RH (ascending) and LH (descending).

— Workout #5 —

Dexterity exercise with frequent changes of direction.

— Workout #5 —

Dexterity exercise with the hands contracting. Play legato throughout, including from measure to measure.

Workout #5

Stability exercise: use only fingers 2, 3, and 4 throughout.

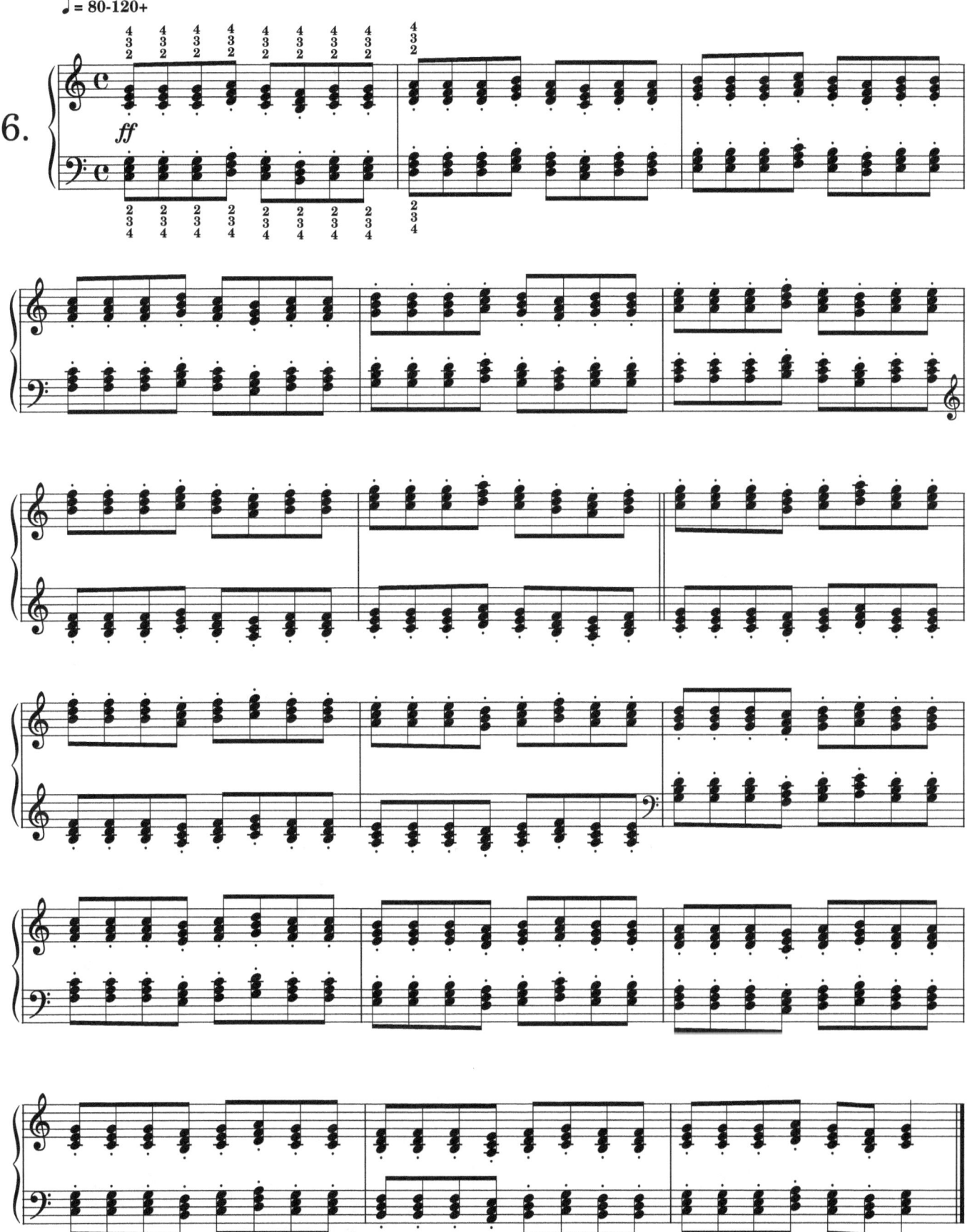

— Workout #5 —

Stability exercise: use only 2-3-5 in the RH and 2-4-5 in the LH throughout.

— Workout #5 —

Stability exercise: use only 2-4-5 in the RH and 2-3-5 in the LH throughout.

177

— Workout #5 —

Exercise for positioning the thumb under the hand.

— Workout #5 —

Exercise for positioning the thumb under the hand.

— Workout #5 —

Stability preparation for ascending melodic minor scales. Follow the fingering carefully.

11.

180

— Workout #5 —

Crossover preparation for ascending melodic minor scales. Follow the fingering carefully, and release the dotted quarter notes early to move to the next position.

— Workout #5 —

One-octave melodic minor scales. Follow the fingering carefully.

13.

182

— Workout #5 —

Two-octave melodic minor scales, ascending. Follow the fingering carefully. (The rests allow time to reset.)

♩. = 112-160+

14.

183

— Workout #5 —

Legato double-neighbor figure in thirds with Chopin's fingering.

— Workout #5 —

Legato thirds using 3-4-5 in the outer voices.

Chromatic minor thirds. Play legato in the outer voices.

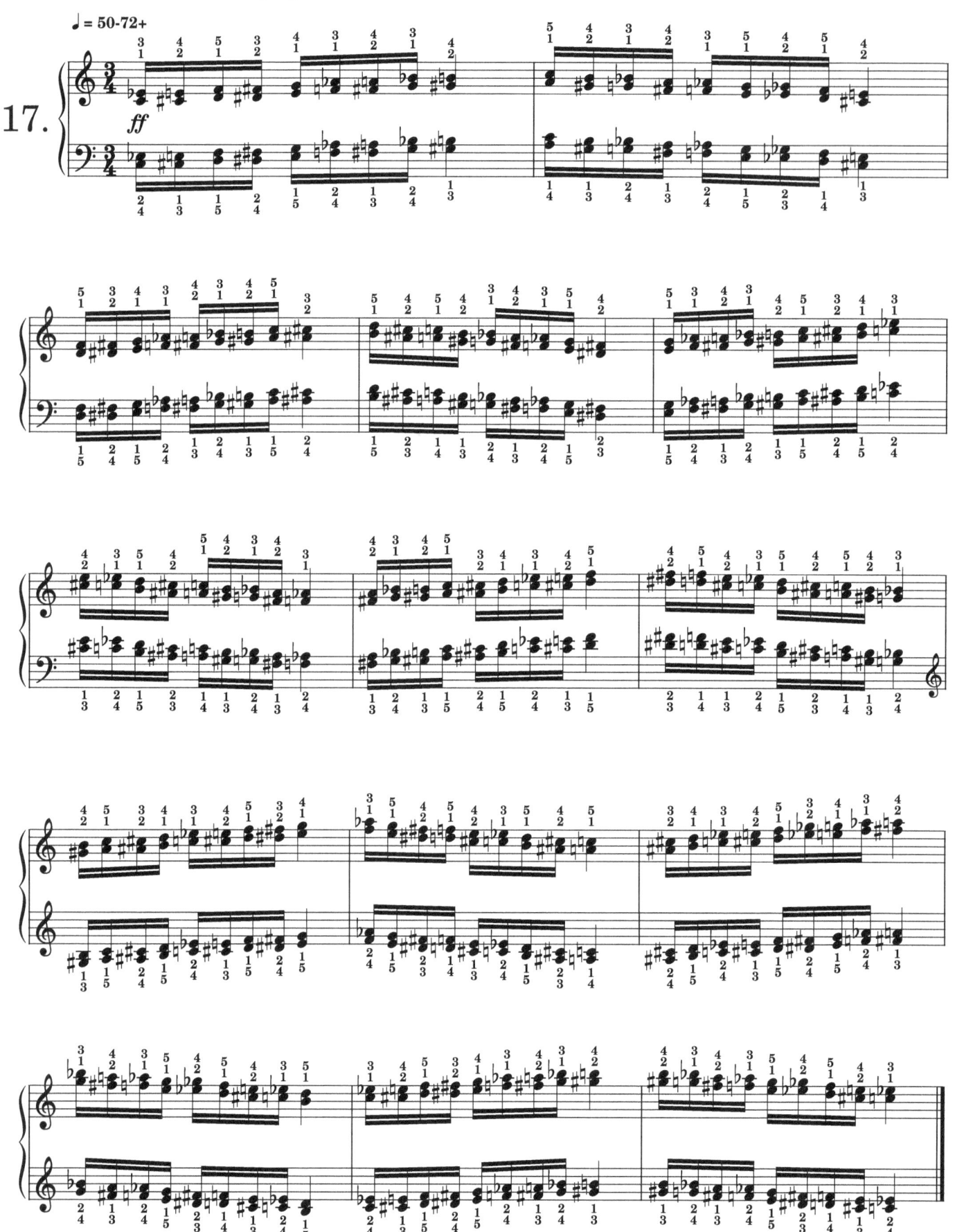

— Workout #5 —

Trill exercise for weaker fingers.

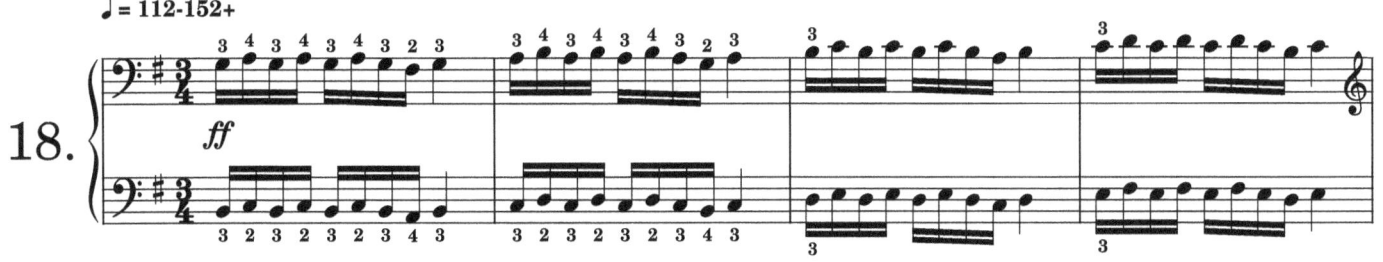

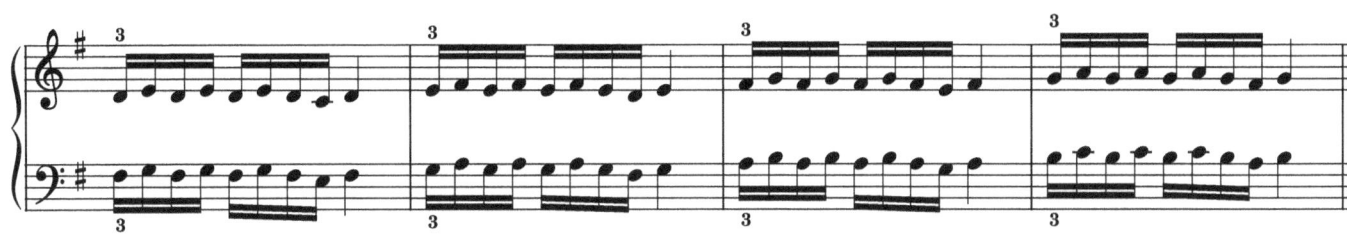

— Workout #5 —

Trill exercise for weaker fingers.

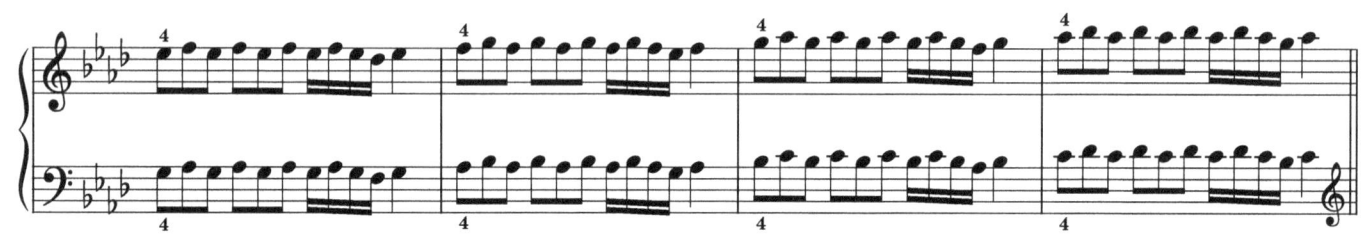

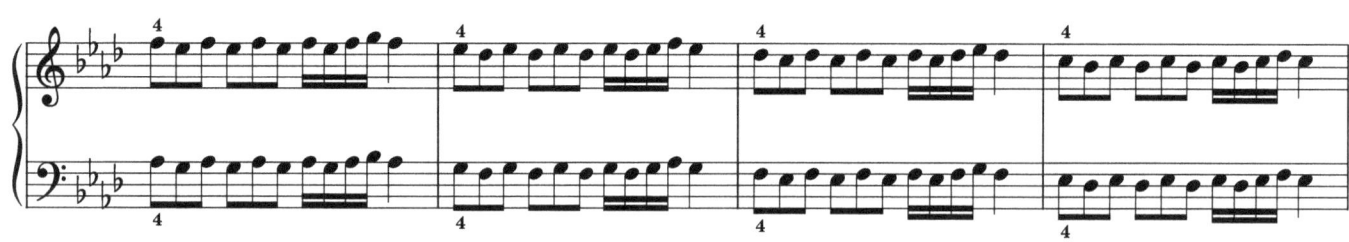
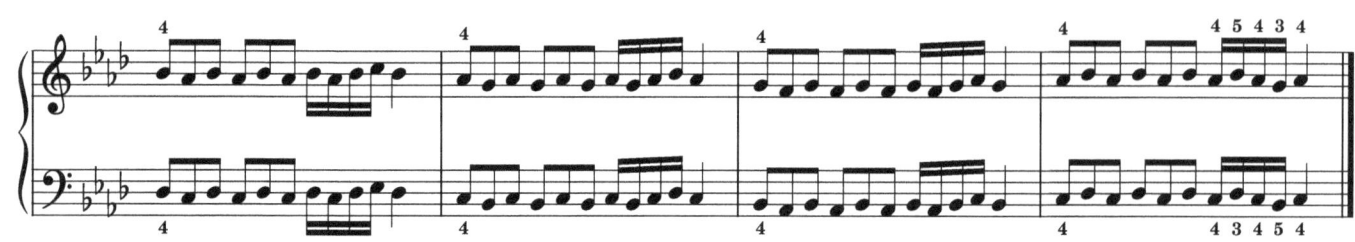

Major scales in 1st-inversion triads. Use the same fingering throughout.

— Workout #5 —

Three-note major triads in all positions. Use the same fingering pattern in all keys.

— Workout #5 —

Double-note exercise with first-inversion triads split between the hands.

— Workout #5 —

Exercise with double notes and emphasis on fingers 4 and 5.

— Workout #5 —

Major arpeggios in octaves. Use the 4th finger on black keys.

— Workout #5 —

Minor arpeggios in octaves. Use the 4th finger on black keys.

— Workout #5 —

Major arpeggios in octaves with changes of direction and larger leaps. Use the 4th finger on black keys.

26. ♩ = 60-120+ *ff*

— Workout #5 —

Dexterity exercise with some contraction of the hand.

— Workout #5 —

Dexterity exercise involving a LH 4-5 stretch (ascending).

— Workout #5 —

Dexterity exercise with frequent changes of direction.

— Workout #5 —

Dexterity exercise with a 2-5 stretch in the RH (ascending) and LH (descending).

— Workout #5 —

Stability preparation for major 7th arpeggios. Follow the fingering carefully.

— Workout #5 —

Crossover preparation for major 7th arpeggios. Follow the fingering carefully.

— Workout #5 —

One-octave major 7th arpeggios. Follow the fingering carefully.

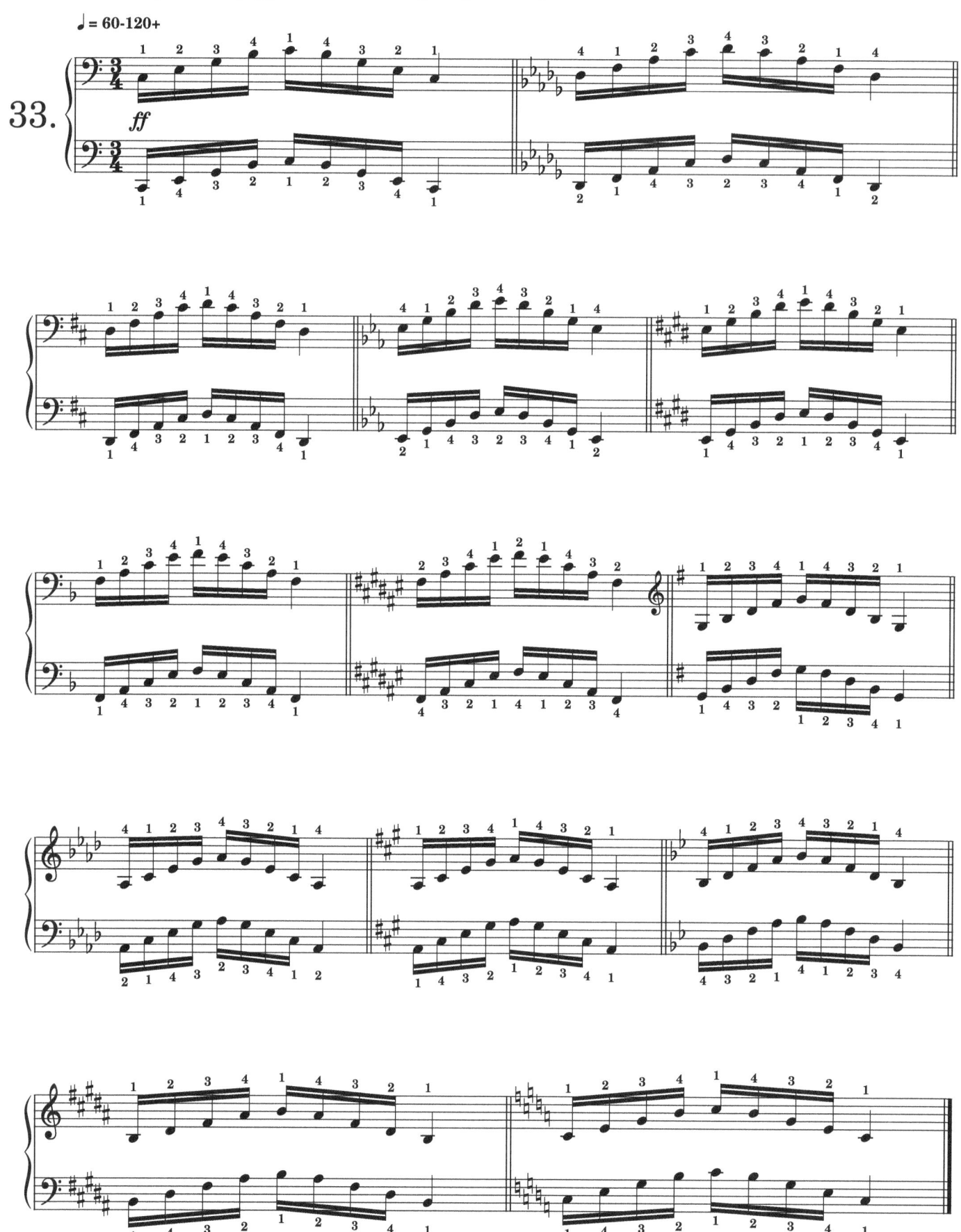

— Workout #5 —

Two-octave major 7th arpeggios. Follow the fingering carefully.

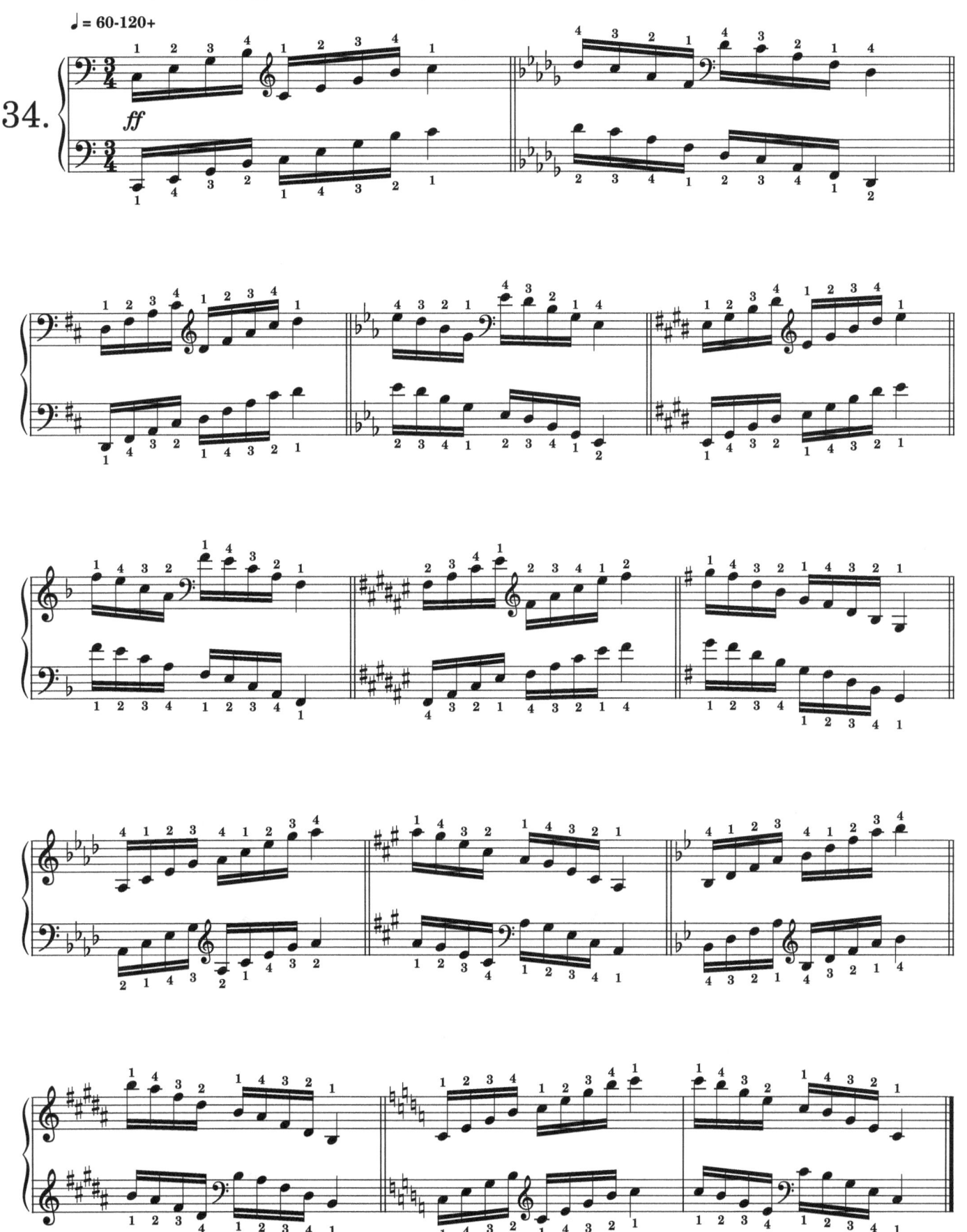

Diminished 7th chords, five notes per hand. Use all five fingers in each hand for all positions.

— Workout #5 —

Cadence formula involving large chords. Use the same fingering pattern in all keys.

— Workout #5 —

Five-note dominant 7th chords. Use all five fingers in each hand for all positions. (Key signatures reflect the root of the chord.)

— Workout #5 —

Five-note broken triads with a span of a 10th. Play legato throughout, including from measure to measure.

— Workout #5 —

Dexterity exercise in contrary motion with focus on the 1-3 octave stretch.

— Workout #5 —

Dexterity exercise in contrary motion with each hand spanning a 10th.

www.ingramcontent.com/pod-product-compliance
Lightning Source LLC
Chambersburg PA
CBHW081223170426
43198CB00017B/2696